# LEADERSHIP AND CULTURE

The Rapid Rise of Chinese Transformational Leadership:
*The Model for the Contemporary Chinese Business Leader (The Study)*

## DR. LIANA C SAENZ

WESTBOW®
PRESS
A DIVISION OF THOMAS NELSON
& ZONDERVAN

Scripture taken from the Holy Bible, NEW INTERNATIONAL VERSION®.
Copyright © 1973, 1978, 1984 by Biblica, Inc. All rights reserved worldwide.
Used by permission. NEW INTERNATIONAL VERSION® and NIV® are
registered trademarks of Biblica, Inc. Use of either trademark for the offering
of goods or services requires the prior written consent of Biblica US, Inc.

WestBow Press books may be ordered through booksellers or by contacting:

WestBow Press
A Division of Thomas Nelson & Zondervan
1663 Liberty Drive
Bloomington, IN 47403
www.westbowpress.com
1 (866) 928-1240

Because of the dynamic nature of the Internet, any web addresses or
links contained in this book may have changed since publication and
may no longer be valid. The views expressed in this work are solely those
of the author and do not necessarily reflect the views of the publisher,
and the publisher hereby disclaims any responsibility for them.

Any people depicted in stock imagery provided by Thinkstock are models,
and such images are being used for illustrative purposes only.
Certain stock imagery © Thinkstock.

ISBN: 978-1-4908-7994-9 (sc)
ISBN: 978-1-4908-7995-6 (hc)
ISBN: 978-1-4908-7993-2 (e)

Library of Congress Control Number: 2015907380

Print information available on the last page.

WestBow Press rev. date: 7/16/2015

# Contents

Dedication ....................................................................... vii
Preface ............................................................................. ix
About the Author .......................................................... xvii
Introduction.................................................................... xxi

### PART I: LEADERSHIP AND CULTURE

1 Leadership........................................................................ 1
        Transformational Leadership ................................... 6
2 Culture............................................................................. 9
        Culture and Leadership ........................................... 12
            Individualism vs. Collectivism............................ 15
        Cross-Cultural Leadership ...................................... 22
            Acculturation ..................................................... 26
3 Transformational Leadership and Collectivism Societies ...... 32
        Factors of Transformational Leadership .......................... 35
            Idealized Influence ............................................. 35
            Inspirational Motivation..................................... 35
            Intellectual Stimulation...................................... 36
            Individual Consideration.................................... 36
        Transformational Leadership Studies and Research ....... 36

### PART II: THE STUDY

4 Synopsis of the Study .................................................... 39
        Introduction ............................................................ 39
        Significance of the Study ......................................... 40
        Chinese Leadership.................................................. 41
        China Today............................................................ 52

Chinese Economy and Leadership in USA......................58
New Generation of Chinese Leaders..............................66
Discussion, Interpretation and Recommendations.........74
Areas for Further Research ...........................................83
Conclusion ..................................................................84
Bibliography................................................................85

# Dedication

To the Leader of leaders, the One who gave me passion and courage, the One who gave me a vision to complement the purpose, and the One who gave me all the challenges and, at the same time, the strength and resources to overcome them. To the Leader who taught me the real meaning of faith, love, trust, influence, and care. Dear Jesus Christ, this journey would not be possible without Your guidance and love every day of my life. I have come this far because of Your grace and by trusting You in every word. When I was tired, You lifted me up; when I was frightened, You held my hand; You helped me grow. What a journey this has been, but through You all things are possible. Thank You for all You have done in my life and throughout my life and for all You will continue to do. I deeply love You.

To my daughters, my everyday motivation and inspiration, Jhoanne and Kimberly, for their love, support, understanding, and patience during these years of my writing journey. I give them my gratitude for all their efforts and sacrifices during this time. Love you, *las lindas!*

# Preface

Living on the West Coast of United States for many years helped me to understand the concepts of acculturation, collectivism, and individualism in societies. Migration from a Latin American country to the United States took me through a practical process of acculturation. The process was not only about the transition from my native culture into the new mosaic of cultures existing in the United States but also included my learning experiences as I observed how acculturation processes operate in different cultures. The phenomenon of acculturation takes place not only in societal cultures but in organizational cultures as well.

As a native of a Latin American country who, at the time of selecting this topic and establishing a hypothesis, had been living in the United States, I expected questions about my choice of subject. My reasons for choosing China and its leaders as the subject for the study have been a recurring point of discussion with the majority of leaders I have interviewed and even with teachers, friends, and family. Furthermore, while I was doing research, I found out that most of the studies done on People's Republic of China have in fact been written by researchers from the eastern side of world and not by Hispanics.

One of the acculturation processes that captured my attention involved the Chinese population living in United States—or more accurately, the Chinese business leaders living and working in the United States. During the same period of time, I became highly interested in the leadership and the social and economic evolution of the People's Republic of China; this was stimulated mainly by my studies in economics and finance as I worked toward my master's degree. I found out that acculturation can exist on a great and complex scale when the process is between collectivistic and individualistic societies or vice versa.

The doctoral dissertation "The Rapid Rise of Chinese Transformational Leadership: The Model for the Contemporary Chinese Business Leader" was a research study I started while I was taking an economics class as part of my master's degree. For this class I prepared a presentation and a paper about the Asia-Pacific Economic Cooperation (APEC)—a group that includes twenty-one members and is predominantly concerned with trade and economic issues concerning their members (APEC, 2014). During this study my attention was particularly drawn to the People's Republic of China and its astonishing development in the last twenty years. I was struck not only by its rise as a global economic player and its evolution into wider global issues but also by its approach to meeting challenges, due largely to the transitions its leaders were facing in having a Communist country with an open market.

I must also admit that other factors also allowed me to observe the acculturation process more closely. Living in Orange County, California, for more than thirteen years and having many multicultural neighbors and communities living close to our house had a strong and positive impact on me as I observed strong family bonds and commercial skills—especially in the Chinese community. I was made especially aware of it when I was able to speak in Spanish and be understood in a pearl shop in Beijing, not to mention that while I was selecting pearls for my necklaces, one of the owners of the shop asked one of my daughters to write down for her, in Spanish, some of the phrases she wanted to use with her Hispanic customers. Of course, as history has shown, there are still cultural differences, but later on, while working and conducting interviews with several business leaders in Shanghai, I had the opportunity to observe many cultural similarities in collectivistic societies; the younger generations particularly were presenting many characteristics of an individualistic society.

As a result, for more than ten years I have been researching and observing the relationship between acculturation and the leadership style/practices of Chinese business leaders living and working in the United States. The ride has been an epic one, with a lot to learn, explore, and discover. It has been a truly worthwhile journey, as the results are giving me an insight into understanding the deep relationship between leadership and culture and, of course, becoming a more aware leader. More than that, it is opening an incredible door of opportunity—the opportunity to share ideas with leaders in the area of culture and acculturation and to support their success around the world.

In fact, as I finished this book, I had been listening to speakers on various panels of the Shared Challenges and Cooperation for Korea, China, and the United States conference—hosted at the end of 2014 by the Brookings Institution's Center for East Asia Policy Studies, with the Korea Foundation for Advanced Studies and Peking University's School of International Studies. What really grabbed my attention was the keynote speaker, Mr. Daniel Russell, assistant secretary of state for the Bureau of East Asian and Pacific Affairs, who talked about the US pivot to the Asia-Pacific area.

Mr. Russell affirmed that President Obama and Secretary Kerry both believe America's well-being, security, prosperity, and future are deeply affected by developments in Northeast Asia. Further, he stated that the Obama administration places tremendous importance on relations with China, Japan, and the Republic of Korea because of the impact that relationships and policies in Northeast Asia have on the region and the world.

He went on to acknowledge that China, Japan, the Republic of Korea, and the United States are major world economies and homes to some of the world's most innovative thinkers and most efficient manufacturers. One of the main reasons for this affirmation is that they invest in each other and maintain a tight financial and supply-chain link. These economies are not only linked by investment capital, however, but also by human capital; over 40 percent of international students in the United States are from Northeast Asia. Similarly, he said, China has risen to become the fifth-most-popular destination for Americans studying abroad. During 2013 there was a significant increase in American students in Japan and Korea. As a result, the blending of cultures and the sharing of knowledge are visible in many areas—from food, film, and music to the conference itself.

China, South Korea, and Japan are major players in the region's security and economy. All three are increasingly active and influential players on the global stage. Therefore, it is of critical importance that there is communication between these economies—as well as with the United States—so as to build on areas where their interests converge and to manage areas where their interests might conflict. Russell declared that far from "Asia for the Asians," the call is now "Asia for the world." It is critical that these three neighboring countries operate in nothing less than a fully cooperative manner, supporting good relations and strong regional order. That includes involvement in APEC, the East Asia Summit, and other ASEAN (Association of Southeast Asian Nations) - centered forum. And of course, it is built on a strong foundation of US alliances and security partnerships that have kept the region safe and stable.

His speech also explained that it is now China's turn but that China's rise is by no means the only development; the entire Asia-Pacific region is changing. India is "Acting East" (more able to cooperate with East); ASEAN is becoming more integrated; Indonesia's democracy is flourishing; and Burma's reformers are pushing forward. America's rebalance is also continuing, and our alliances are growing stronger and more capable.

Mr. Russell's discourse did not avoid the current situation in North Korea. He acknowledged that changing dynamics also drive some tensions. North Korea is the dangerous outlier in Asia and is causing the greatest threat in the region. The good news, he said, is that North Korea is an area where the United States and the rest of Northeast Asia cooperate closely. The broad alignment in strategic interests and strategy come from a commitment to cooperation between Beijing, Seoul, Washington, and Tokyo—and Russia as well. They are united on the denuclearization of the Korean peninsula because of the risks posed to all of us by the Democratic People's Republic of Korea's (DRPK) pursuit of nuclear weapons and ballistic missiles, its rejection of international obligations, its broken promises, and its sudden provocations.

In conclusion, Daniel Russell stressed that we have entered the age of networks. Essentially, given our commonalities, it is natural that we should seek opportunities to interact and collaborate; perhaps there is no other choice. The major Northeast Asian powers and the United States need each other—just as much as the rest of the world needs us—to jump-start the global economy, preserve regional stability, enhance global security, and protect the global environment.

## *The Study*

The result of this research is a quantitative and qualitative study using a two-phase sequential mixed method, integrating numerical data and text. The analysis focuses on the correlation between acculturation scores, demographics (independent variables), and leadership styles/practices (dependent variables). The quantitative method includes two assessments: the SL-ASIA scale and the Multifactor Leadership Questionnaire 5X (MLQ-5X).

The findings of this study, which became a doctoral dissertation, suggest that acculturation scores have a significant correlation with leadership style/practices and, further, that a relationship exists between acculturation scores determined by the Suinn-Lew Asian Self Identity Acculturation scale (SL-ASIA) and the leadership style/practices of the business leaders as defined by the Multifactor Leadership Questionnaire (MLQ-5X).

In greater detail, chapter 1 of the study provides background and an explanation of the problem to be addressed, the purpose of the study, the guiding research questions and hypothesis, the limitations and delimitations, the definitions of terms, and the significance of the study.

Then in chapter 2, the study incorporates the theoretical support for the study. This literature review examines global, Western-dominated, cross-cultural, transactional and transformational, servant, and organizational leadership as an aid to comprehending leadership theory and establishing general leadership characterization. An inspection of Chinese traditional and contemporary leadership, including major leaders and their philosophies, has been included for a deeper understanding of the cultural and political aspects of Chinese business leaders and the evolution of their leadership style. The literature review also addresses contemporary China, including the market economy, leadership development, international affairs, and population—issues that are affecting the evolution of Chinese business leaders. Further, chapter 2 includes an examination of the Chinese economy and leadership in the United States and considers acculturation, in order to understand the experience of Chinese business leaders in the United States. Finally, the chapter inspects the new generation of Chinese business leaders.

Chapter 3 of the study contains the research design, instrumentation, research sample, procedures, sequential mix method data collection, data processing and analysis, research ethics, and methodological assumptions and limitations. Chapter 4 presents the research question and hypothesis; a description of the sample; data collection - phases one and two; quantitative data analysis; qualitative data analysis; and quantitative-qualitative data analysis. Chapter 5 of the study contains discussion, a conclusion, and recommendations.

The study recommends the design of a specific scale exclusively for a Chinese population that allows a more accurate acculturation assessment and understanding of Chinese business leaders living and working in the United States. The research also suggests further studies to investigate the relationship between acculturation and the leadership style/practices of Chinese business leaders living and working in the United States. This incorporates larger distribution areas of the Chinese population in the United States, as well as a broader spectrum of companies that represent more sectors of the US economy.

The current lack of literature on the relationship between acculturation and leadership for Chinese business leaders in the United States allows this study a unique perspective and the opportunity to establish new ground based on its empirical findings. Both a synopsis of the study and its findings are reported in chapter 4 of this book.

In brief, the study has greatly increased my awareness and interest in comprehending the attributes of transformational leaders and, further, the components of the relationship between transformational leadership and collectivistic societies. Of course, this approach does not suggest that this is a perfect match, but history has shown that these two elements—transformational leadership and collectivistic societies—interrelate in a way that can make a remarkable and effective contribution to leadership effectiveness.

## The Book

For years now, running parallel with my research and study has been my own experience in "corporate America." I have worked with companies in a range of industries—from governments to Global 500 companies. I have also offered my services, working as a volunteer and leading other volunteers in not-for-profit organizations in multicultural settings.

While writing this book, I was involved in teaching, mentoring, and coaching leaders in a diverse environment, as well as designing, developing and directing a multicultural program designed to enhance intercultural awareness in a multinational corporation.

All of these experiences have inspired me to continue my research and study. I want to continue learning and understanding the components that shape the relationship between leadership and culture; I am keen to increase intercultural awareness, and most importantly, I want to develop better ways to apply it.

The success of today's global leaders and organizations depends on the level of intercultural awareness and perspective on diversity, as well as the correct application of knowledge and intercultural skills. Multicultural teams, organizations, and individuals have opportunities to develop strategies that provide better solutions, increase productivity, improve communications, build teams and communities, and naturally bring economic benefits to organizations and individuals. Good leadership and cultural awareness are their most important resources.

An understanding of Chinese business leaders is probably more important than ever. Increased globalization means greater networking between East and West; alliances and collaboration will play a major role in all economies in the next century. Globalization requires an understanding of not only Chinese business leaders but also leaders around the globe. Understanding more about the culture and leadership characteristics of Chinese business leaders, however, is definitely a great start.

In brief, this book starts with an introduction to leadership and culture; it then expands further the topics of cultural dimensions, acculturation, and transformational leadership. The final chapter includes some fundamental elements of the doctoral dissertation, "The Rapid Rise of Chinese Transformational Leadership: The Model for the Contemporary Chinese Business Leader," and other selected portions of the study.

Enjoy!

# About the Author

The understanding that every one of us was born to lead has driven Dr. Saenz's passion for leadership and culture. She believes that leadership is about influence, and the ability we all have to connect our given strengths and talents to a bigger purpose.

The belief which inspires her is that influence that has a clear purpose can be exerted anywhere and under any circumstances; an influencer need not have a title or a professional position. A leader's influence makes its first appearance at home, is extended to family and friends, and can benefit the workplace, the community, and wider society. Influence has changed the world and has transformed people - and will continue to do so.

Dr. Saenz was born in Bogota, Colombia, and most of her ancestors were also from Colombia. From an early age she developed an interest in cultural differences and similarities. She took every opportunity to gain knowledge, understanding and personal experience of the close relationship between leadership and culture. She recalls a particular occasion during her student years when she took part in a student leaders' movement to guide an initiative that became the referendum that resulted in the transformation of the political constitution of Colombia - the current governing document of the Republic of Colombia. It is better known as the Constitution of 1991, promulgated on July 4, and replacing the Constitution of 1886. It has recently been called the Constitution of Rights. This opportunity to lead students and citizens towards a vision for a nation that works together for a common purpose was a real starting point. She became more acutely aware of the need for leadership at all levels, and understood more clearly the importance of the role that culture plays in the way individuals, organizations, and society in general, can be influenced.

After finishing a Bachelor of Arts degree, Dr. Saenz immigrated to the United States and settled on the West Coast. It was during these years that she came to understand indeed the meaning of the concepts of acculturation, collectivism and individualism in societies. As an immigrant from a Latin American country she herself experienced the process of acculturation and gained tremendous insight into cultural awareness and how leadership, and culture, and the relationship between them greatly influence the ability to lead in a multicultural environment.

During the past 25 years she has also experienced "corporate America" in a range of industries - from government to Global 500 companies - in a multicultural environment. In observing managers and leaders, she has seen how those who exercise cultural awareness and understand the power of leadership are effective, efficient, and better able to build confidence and trust. They know how to empower and influence people, resulting in personal and economic growth and a higher level of team experience and success. On the other hand, she also witnessed the inability of some managers to understand the value of leading people to success; she saw managers of multinational corporations who simply had no cultural awareness and had not develop their leadership capabilities; as a result, their management faced many internal conflicts, which lowered morale. The result is a corporate culture that achieves tasks by employing the threat of punishment, rather than by motivating people to create opportunities; this, in turn, leads to low employee retention rates.

In summary, Dr. Saenz has observed the significance and implications of managing with no leadership abilities and cultural intelligence. The result is a negative environment characterized by unproductive relationships and weak team development. Such managers are deficient in obtaining information, poor at handling discrepancies, and lacking in the capacity to build agreements. There is poor, and slow, decision-making within the organization and in relation to customers, which leads to personal resentment.

During her master and doctoral studies Dr. Saenz lived mainly in the United States, spending periods of time in Asia and Latin America. As a result, she has reached a point in the acculturation process where she feels comfortable living in cultures with different values, assumptions, beliefs and behaviors. Her accumulated experiences have helped her observe, through a different lens, the concepts of leadership and culture and the effects of culture on the practice of leadership, with all its implications.

Dr. Saenz has more than ten years of experience as a servant-leader volunteering and leading volunteers in not-for-profit organizations. She has also spent considerable time as a serious student, researcher and writer in the areas of leadership, culture, Chinese business leaders, and transformational and servant leadership. All of this, as well as her roles in teaching, mentoring, coaching and helping both individuals and teams in multicultural environments to achieve success, has allowed her to observe and study transformational leaders and their power of influence and change in different cultures. She could not be better placed to recognize, and agree with many researchers and leadership practitioners, that there is a pressing need for a better understanding of the connection and implications of leadership and culture links and application.

She has observed that, without cultural awareness, there is inevitably misunderstanding and an underestimation of values, beliefs and ways of doing things. The lack of understanding of how cultural differences impact our judgment and ability to relate to and influence others, significantly changes the way we think, judge, act and react; this can be devastating in relationships, whether in a family or personal setting, or in a workplace or business.

Dr. Saenz profoundly believes that the understanding of our own and others' behaviors and their cultural perspectives are vital for effective work, communication and negotiation. The ability to present ourselves effectively, to build credibility, to connect with and to influence others is the cornerstone of leadership in a global environment.

# Introduction

Globalization is no longer a choice of certain companies or corporations; globalization is a trend in everybody's life. Are you connected to the world? The Internet has changed how we meet people, have conversations, and spend time with others. Our lives are no longer influenced only by the ones closest to our rooms, houses, or workplaces. We are connecting daily with the rest of the world.

As of March 1, 2015, out of the 7.3 billion total people in the world 3.0 billion are Internet users, 2.1 billion are active social media users, and 7.1 billion are mobile subscribers. Further, according to Ericsson's 2015 mobility report the number of mobile broadband subscriptions will increase by 5.4 billion by 2020. As you are reading these lines, there are thousands of new users of the Internet developing new ways to communicate and connect to others. Further, it is without doubt that a variety of new cultures are developing on the Internet as the world becomes a village and the Internet becomes the place where billions meet every day. I dare to say that the eighth continent is not a pile of garbage in some far place or Atlantis. The eighth continent is the Internet, with 3.0 billion or more inhabitants. All of these data illustrate that globalization, like never before, has required that we embrace a higher level of understanding of each other's culture and values, regardless of our physical location in the world. As we are getting interconnected with the rest of the planet and aim to thrive socially, economically, intellectually, and professionally, it is more than evident that we need to increase our cultural awareness. It does not matter how physically far we are from each other—we as humans want to relate, connect, influence, and transform others.

Is the impact of global communications increasing our desire to extend our frontiers? Globalization has not only affected us socially and culturally; it has had an impact on the world economy as well. Business globalization has caused executives around the globe to aspire to become global leaders with abilities to influence people across cultural and national boundaries and excel at global innovation. Many have noticed, and researchers have recognized it: cultural forces influence many aspects of leadership.

If this is your first examination into the topics of leadership and culture, most likely you would like to know what leadership and culture are. Perhaps you would like to know if you are a leader and, furthermore, understand how leadership and culture relate. Leadership and culture are universal topics that have existed from the beginning of human history and have been studied for centuries. However, leadership is often misunderstood. It's been confused with management, entrepreneurship, intelligence, knowledge, pioneers, and of course, a title or position of responsibility or power. Moreover, being a leader has been confused with having the ability to lead. Culture has been similarly misinterpreted and mislabeled as ethnicity, diversity, and stereotypes, and a blend between national, ethnic, and organizational culture. Regrettably, the study of culture has focused more on our differences than our similarities.

Now, if you are well-versed on the topics of leadership and culture, you most likely will agree with the fact that leadership and culture are strongly related. If we would like to be successful in the fast speed of globalization and connect to influence others around the world, leadership and culture are inseparable subjects. In fact, I truly believe that a leader without cultural awareness and global leadership skills is not able to lead to his or her full potential—not in the global arena and not in today's world.

Leaders should be able to answer questions such as the following: Can we really lead without cultural awareness? How do cultural attributes facilitate leadership influence? Can leaders effectively influence without understanding someone's cultural values, assumptions, and beliefs? All these questions are absolutely worthy to be answered in the minds of unstoppable globalization. Global leaders recognize the need to develop their cultural awareness to be able to lead in a globalized society. Globalization is not an option; it's a trend. It is a fact that building organizations and teams in a multicultural environment can quickly become unproductive where there is no cultural awareness. Culture has an influence on building agreements, establishing productive relationships, developing teams, obtaining information, handling discrepancies,, and making decisions within organizations and with customers.

A leader's influence is effective to the extent of his or her level of cultural awareness. We have to recognize that we are far from the final conclusions on the topics of leadership and culture as they evolved as humans does; as culture evolved, leadership has to be to fine-tuned and vice versa. Consequently, we must continue researching, observing, and learning from the global cultural behaviors that are facilitating leadership effectiveness in a globalized world.

# 1

## Leadership

Leadership is the fundamental nature of humanity. Yet not every person understands this gift or achieves control over it. Do you know that no one is born without the ability to lead, to influence, to change, to serve, and to transform others? It may sound like rhetoric, but yes, you are a leader. Many people do not believe or feel they are leaders who can further develop their leadership capabilities. Some even deny they are leaders. During my teaching times in conferences, seminars, and so forth, I have observed the reactions of participants when I called them leaders or asked the leaders to raise their hands. Not all of them did it. Some people clarify they are not leaders, because they are not in charge of others or they are not managers in their jobs yet.

Ken Blanchard and Phil Hodges, founders of Lead Like Jesus©®, explained in detail why many people don't know that they are leaders. People have personal definitions and images of a leader. For many people, the word *leader* correlates with someone who has a position of responsibility and/or a formal title, such as captain, president, or director. A basic Web search helps us to better understand this issue. Society in general sees a leader as someone who commands a formal organization, group, or country. A basic search for the word in encyclopedias and dictionaries says a leader is someone who leads, but they further accentuate it as a person who directs a military force or unit; a person who has commanding authority or influence; the principal officer of a British political party; a party member chosen to manage party activities in a legislative body; a party member presiding over the whole legislative body when the party constitutes a majority; or a first or principal performer of a group, to mention a few. In reality, the term *leader* has been underestimated and poorly discussed, understood, and applied.

Leaders and leadership have been present since the beginning of creation. In fact, leadership was given to humanity after the creation of the universe. The first book of the Bible, Genesis, in chapter 1, clearly shows that God, the leader of leaders, created humans in His own image and commanded man and woman to have dominion over the earth (Gen. 1:26 NIV). God creates leadership, calls believers to lead others, and provides the best compendium of leadership ever written that humankind can find: the Bible. All leadership principles, "have been woven into it by the One who invented leadership," as stated by John Maxwell in his leadership Bible. I truly believe this.

In today's studies, research, and organizational sciences, leadership is one of the most scrutinized subjects, with thousands of pages written in books, academic journals, business-oriented magazines, and general-interest periodicals (Luthans, 2005). The study of leadership has roots in the beginning of civilization. Egyptian rulers, Greek heroes, and biblical patriarchs all have one thing in common—leadership (Stone and Patterson, 2005).

The word *leadership* in Egyptian hieroglyphic symbols has existed for at least five thousand years (Bass, 1990). One of the oldest books, *The Teachings of Ptah-Hotep,* dates from 2388 BC. Ptah-Hotep was an Egyptian city administrator, and in this book he incorporates moral teachings and the correct way to lead. Yet in the English language, the word *leadership* is surprisingly a new addition. It appeared approximately two hundred years ago in writings about political influence in the British Parliament (House et al., 2004).

Conversely, the definition of leadership among scholars is not unanimous (Bass, 1990; Yukl, 2002). There is doubt in the accurate characterization of leadership, even with an abundance of works in the literature. Leadership correlates with major criterion variables like subordinate satisfaction, commitment, and performance to the point where the concept of leadership has remained an inexplicable idea and generally remains in a black box (Luthans, 2005). Some scholars delineated leadership as the process by which a person influences others to accomplish an objective and directs the organization in a way that makes it more cohesive and coherent (Wren, 1995; Flood, 2010). Leaders carry out this process by applying their leadership attributes, such as beliefs, values, ethics, character, knowledge, and skills (Flood, 2010).

One of the most important studies in the last decades, the Global Leadership and Organizational Behavior Effectiveness (GLOBE), is a study of sixty-two societies. It was designed to explore the relationship among organizational and societal culture and the content of culturally endorsed implicit theories of leadership (CLTs) (House et al., 2004), which surpasses all other research studies, including Hofstede's 1980 study, in scope, depth, length, and complexity (Grove, 2005). It provides many theoretical and methodological contributions, developing an integrated theory "of the relationship between cultural values and practices and leadership, organizational, and societal effectiveness" (House et al., 2004, p. 724). House et al. suggested the definition of *leadership* involves influence on leaders to help others and defined leadership as "the ability of an individual to influence, motivate, and enable others to contribute toward the effectiveness and success of the organization of which they are members" (p. 15).

John Maxwell, author of "The 21 Irrefutable Laws of Leadership," defined leadership as "influence nothing more nothing else," further explaining that "leadership is not about titles, positions or flowcharts. It is about one life influencing another." Ken Blanchard writes, "Leadership is an influence process. Any time you seek to influence the thinking, behavior, or development of another person toward the accomplishment of a goal or purpose." Other scholars have defined leadership as the way for people to contribute to making something extraordinary happen (Chemers, 2002; Kouzes and Posner, 2007).

In addition, the definition of leadership is usually extended to the leader and his or her capabilities. It has been said as well that leadership not only establishes relationships among leaders and followers who propose to effect genuine changes, mirroring their shared intentions (Rost, 1993), but is not what leaders do; rather, leadership is what leaders and followers do simultaneously for the collective good (Rost, 1993).

In many leadership research investigations, the focus is on the leader's personality, previous actions, or decisions. However, the emphasis has shifted to leadership style (Keller, 1999). Leadership style figures more prominently in effective organizations, where it is defined as the "characteristic manner in which a person behaves in attempting to influence the actions or beliefs of others, particularly subordinates" (Robinson, 1993, p. 7).

Further, leadership needs to be differentiated from management, as suggested by Grint (2002). He also explained the art of management involves planning, organizing, directing, and controlling. He defined a manager as the person who carries out these functions. A leader influences, while a manager possesses formal authority by virtue of his or her position or profession. An effective leader is not necessarily a good manager. A manager's formal authority or position is not a key factor of a leader's ability to influence others (Van Wart, 2003).

Stephen Covey in 1990 acknowledged management is not leadership; they are two concepts, and leadership has to come first and deal with decisions. Covey further explained leadership concentrates on the things to accomplish, while management fundamentally focuses on how to best accomplish certain things. In other words, "management is efficient in climbing the ladder of success; leadership determines whether the ladder is leaning against the right wall" (p. 101).

The study of leadership in the course of history is remarkable. Plato declared in 423 BC, "The wise shall lead and rule, and the ignorant shall follow." Then Sun Tzu, in 560 BC, introduced *The Art of War* and its military principles. Machiavelli's *The Prince*, in 1450, brought us, "The end justifies the means," and, "Keep your friends close and your enemies closer."

In the West, the main theories and approaches toward leadership in the early days stemmed from the literature of Adam Smith, whose *The Wealth of Nations* (1776) discussed the benefits of leading and following. Georg W. F. Hegel's *The First Book of Leadership* (1807) focused on leadership in the political process. Thomas Carlyle's great man theory argued that leaders are born. Then the trait theory argued that effective leaders share a number of common personality characteristics or "traits." Then Stogdill argued in 1948 that leaders are not born; it is the situation that creates them. Max Weber's charismatic leadership (1950) claimed leaders emerge in a time of crisis due to charisma. McGregor's 1960 theory X and Y described two leaders—a lazy one motivated only by extrinsic rewards and a hard worker who wanted to do a good job. Fieldler's contingency theory (1970) suggested two types of leaders: those who focus on task and those who focus on relationships. Also in the seventies Hersey and Blanchard's situational leadership argued that is not best way to lead because leaders will adjust accordingly. Greenleaf's servant leadership (1977) argued that in the corporate environment, the leadership role is most successful if leaders serve those they lead. Then James McGregor, Burn, and Bass's transactional leadership (1978) argued transactions are made between leaders and followers for mutual benefit, and transformational leadership stated in 1985 that the interaction in a solid relationship allows leaders to transform followers.

Main non-Western leadership theories and approaches include Sinha in India, who in 1980 developed the nurturant-task model, where the ideal leader is both nurturant and task oriented. Misumi's 1985 research in Japan on performance maintenance identified four types of leaders classified by the two basic leadership functions, performance, and maintenance. This theory was adapted later in China, but character and morals were added as leadership functions. In 1985, Al-Kubaisy, from the Arab Gulf countries, combined family, tribal, and bureaucratic structures for a leadership style characterized by a patriarchal approach, with strong hierarchical authority and subordination to laws based on the personality and power of those who make them.

As previously stated, transactional and transformational leadership are the latest and most promising phases of leadership theory. Research shows transformational leadership has universality, as can be found in all parts of the globe and all forms of organizations (Bass 1997). Research on transformational leadership from the GLOBE study supports that charismatic-transformational leadership has valued leadership qualities in all countries and cultures. Furthermore, research using the Multifactor Leadership Questionnaire (MLQ) has taken place on every continent and in almost every industrialized country. In the same fashion, research suggests transformational leadership not only provides a positive augmentation in leader performance but also transformational leadership should be a more effective type of leadership around the world, as the ability of transformational leadership to transcend its own self-interest and work toward the common goal of others can impact all cultures and organizations (Burns, 1978). Let's observe transformational leadership closely.

## *Transformational Leadership*

Transformational leadership is more than a leadership theory; it is a journey, as the elements that make a transformational leader really go above and beyond personal interest. A transformational leader is one who commits himself or herself first by creating an atmosphere of self-awareness, which is a key element of any leader's success. Then the leader shows personal dedication to each person, developing trust and connections; then comes loyalty to the family or the groups to which the leader belongs, creating a sense of teams and community; and then comes the pledge to the leader's community or the organizations, creating unity and increasing the levels of effectiveness and continuous growth.

Bass and Avolio (1994) described transformational leadership as "an expansion of transactional leadership" (p. 3). Van Seters and Field the previous year inferred that the dramatic improvement of transformational leadership over all previous theories is that it is based on intrinsic rather than extrinsic motivation. Leaders must be proactive rather than reactive in their thinking, radical rather than conservative, and open to new ideas and more creative and innovative (Bass, 1985). Transformational leadership is useful and valuable in producing and maintaining organizational changes.

As the definition implies, transformational leadership goes beyond focusing on the exchange between leaders and followers to a more extensive standpoint, including raising the interests of employees, inspiring workers to look further than their own interests to what would benefit the group, and cheering employees to acknowledge the organization's undertakings as their own (Sanders, Hopkins, & Geroy, 2003). Transformational leaders may use numerous techniques in accomplishing their objectives, such as stimulating employees by using the power of charisma exclusively, appealing to an employee's emotional needs, or stimulating employees intellectually (Sanders et al., 2003).

As affirmed by Burns in 1978, transformational leaders ask followers to surpass their own self-interest for the good of the group, organization, or society; to consider their long-term needs to develop themselves rather than their immediate needs; and to become more aware of what is really important. Thus, through this interaction, followers are converted into leaders. Associates' confidence levels rise, and their needs broaden from leadership that encourages growth to a higher potential. This special motivation is linked to empirically derived factors of transformational leadership, which we will study in detail in chapter 3.

Leadership is a worldwide concept as all human beings born with the ability to lead. Yet, there are many perspectives on leadership, and its practice differs in every part of the world (CCL, 2010). Leadership has an "I know when I see it" feel (House et al., 2004, p. 51), and it can be sometimes an ambiguous matter.

The fact that leadership practices differ in every part of the world makes it crucial to add to any leadership study a cross-cultural lens. So, let's take a little walk down the road of the perception of culture.

# 2

## Culture

Culture has been studied for centuries, with anthropologists and behavioral scientists defining culture as the full range of learned human behavior patterns. Have you ever thought about how people from different parts of the world have many similarities, especially nowadays as we communicate globally through the web, yet they continue to maintain their differences?

According to Dennis O'Neil, professor emeritus of the Anthropology Behavioral Sciences Department at Palomar College San Marcos, California, culture is a powerful human tool for survival, but it is a fragile phenomenon. O'Neil further explains that even our written languages, governments, buildings, and other man-made things are merely the products of culture. Culture is "to a human collectivity what personality is to an individual" (Hofstede, 2001 p. 21). The GLOBE study defined culture as "shared motives, values, beliefs, identities, and interpretations or meanings of significant events that result from common experiences of members of collectives that are transmitted across generations" (p. 15). Cultural attributes and definitions have the same meaning for social and organizational structure and analysis, as described by House et al. in the GLOBE study. In an organization's structure, culture is illustrated by the use of nomenclature, shared values, and history. At the societal structure, culture is represented by language and an ideological belief system such as religion, political systems, ethnic heritage, and history. "We are all creatures of culture" (Trompenaars and Hampden-Turner p. 243, 2012)

There is communication between all countries because of the web and economic globalization, which have allowed us to cross distances at an incredible speed. Every day we are closer and closer to the rest of the world. Every day we are exposed to citizens of other continents, far away from home. In a sense sometimes we feel like all the earth becomes one big neighborhood. Yet, cultural differences have not disappeared; in fact, cultural differences will not disappear.

The Bible clearly explains that God divided humans for their own good. It all started with the Tower of Babel, when people decided to go in their own direction instead of obeying God. Because of this God divided people into many languages and groups and scattered them over the face of the whole earth (Gen. 11:9 NIV). From one man God made all nations, so they should inhabit the whole earth, and He marked out their appointed times in history and the boundaries of their lands (Acts 17:26 NIV).

The perception of our identity is different in individualist and collectivist cultures. As individualist cultures focus on independence, collectivist cultures focus on interdependency. People define themselves according to their connection and expression to the social context. In individualist cultures, people try to find a way to be unique or "express the self" while in collectivist cultures, people try to find a way to fit in or to find a place in the social order.

In countries like the United States, where in the majority of the cities your neighbors are from different parts of the world and you attend school and work every day with people native to different continents, you develop an awareness that people have their own perceptions and see things from a unique perspective. The definition of "normal" greatly varies from one person to another. Anyone's beliefs and values (as explained by Hampden-Turner and Trompenaars in 2000) can be challenged when another person does something unexpected and you do not understand the other person's logic. You feel shut out, or you are 100 percent confident that your way to do things is the best.

Value judgments are in place when you are dealing with different cultures, and unknown value systems that would deny your beliefs and values may put what is precious to you in danger. Trompenaars and Hampden-Turner again in 2012 gave us a good example with American-French interactions, which are mainly doomed to failure because both desire to control the environment; there's nothing wrong with this approach, but sometimes it leads to disaster when you put those two together.

One of the most critical challenges that globalization opens for businesses and organizations is the acknowledgement and appreciation of cultural values, practices, and subtleties in people from different parts of the world. Globalization does not mean cultural differences are disappearing or diminishing; on the contrary, as economic borders come down, cultural barriers can go up, presenting new challenges and opportunities to businesses and organizations. "When cultures come into contact, they may converge in some aspects, but their idiosyncrasies will likely amplify" (House et al. 2004).

Indeed, the practice of adapting to other cultures has been the subject of study and advice for centuries. Around AD 55, the apostle Paul illustrated this very well in one of his letters to the Corinthians: "Though I am free and belong to no one, I make myself a slave to everyone, to win as many as possible. To the Jews I became like a Jew, to win the Jews. To those under the law I became like one under the law (though I myself am not under the law), so as to win those under the law. To those not having the law I became like one not having the law (though I am not free from God's law but am under Christ's law), so as to win those not having the law. To the weak I became weak, to win the weak. I have become all things to all people so that by all possible means I might save some. I do all this for the sake of the gospel that I may share in its blessings"

(1 Corinthians 9:19–23 NIV). Then in chapter 10, he wrote: "So whether you eat or drink or whatever you do, do it all for the glory of God. Do not cause anyone to stumble, whether Jews, Greeks or the church of God— even as I try to please everybody in every way. For I am not seeking my own good but the good of many, so that they may be saved" (1 Corinthians 10:31–33 NIV). Let's take a closer look at the relationship between leadership and culture.

## Culture and Leadership

On the other hand, research has shown that there are aspects of leadership comparable across cultures as culture-specific differences in leadership. House et al. in the inferred GLOBE study supported the divergent views of leadership and further stressed that the cross-cultural lens makes it more complex and frightening. Cross-cultural leadership substantiates that leadership cannot be fully observed and practiced without the awareness of how cultural values highly influence its practice and outcome. To what extent is leadership culturally contingent? Are cultural differences in leadership practices the exception or the rule? Are cultural differences here to stay, or will the forces of globalization eventually blur differences among nations?

There are many questions about leadership and culture that research and practice still need to fully address. In today's world, these topics are in great need of understanding, especially when we are facing globalization. Out of the 7.3 billion habitants of earth, 3.0 billion are Internet users, seven times the population of the United States today.

Experts in international business agree that to succeed in global business, business leaders and managers need the flexibility to respond positively and effectively to practices and values totally different from what they are accustomed to. In essence, a substantial amount of empirical research (House, Wright, & Aditya, 1997) has shown that as a result of the cultural forces in the countries or regions in which the leaders function, the status and influence of leaders varies considerably. In fact, the GLOBE study highlights the following:

> Americans, Arabs, Asians, English, Easter European, French, Germans, Latin Americans, and Russians tend to romanticize the concept of leadership and consider leadership in both political and organizational arenas to be important. In these cultures leaders are commemorated with statues, names of major avenues or boulevards, or names of buildings. Many people in German speaking Switzerland, the Netherlands, and Scandinavia are skeptical about leaders and the concept of leadership for fear that they will accumulate and abuse power. In these countries it is difficult to find public commemoration of leaders. (p. 5)

Furthermore, global business communications and economic globalization are taking society to a higher level of interaction, and the need to understand cultural differences in leadership has never been greater. The ability to work in cross-cultural groups is vital to be successful. As well explained by the GLOBE study, there are compelling reasons for considering the role of societal and organizational culture in influencing leadership and organizational processes. There is a need for leadership theories that go above and beyond cultures, yet there is an inherent limitation in applying theories across cultures. "What functions effectively in one culture may not in another culture" (House et al., 2004; Laurent, 1983; Trompenaars, 1993).

Global research on leadership, including societal and organizational cultures, is one of the most important additions to cross-cultural leadership studies. The first significant question elaborated on by the GLOBE study concerned the differentiating attributes of societal and organizational cultures. Thus, GLOBE extended the current knowledge of cultural dimensions, validating nine cultural dimensions, and further conceptualized and measured culture in terms of practices and values (House et al., 2004). After running a questionnaire of 735 items in two pilot studies with middle managers, the GLOBE nine core cultural dimensions are as follows:

1. *Power distance*—expecting and agreeing that power should be stratified and concentrated in higher levels
2. *Institutional collectivism*—encouraging and rewarding collective distribution of resources and collective actions
3. *In-group collectivism*—expressing pride, loyalty, and cohesiveness in organizations or families
4. *Uncertainty avoidance*—avoiding uncertainty by relying on established social norms, rituals, and bureaucratic practices
5. *Gender egalitarianism*—minimizing gender differences and roles and promoting gender equality
6. *Performance orientation*—encouraging and rewarding group members for performance improvement and excellence
7. *Assertiveness*—being self-assured, confrontational, and aggressive in social relationships
8. *Future orientation*—engaging in future-oriented behaviors, such as planning, investing in the future, and delaying individual or collective gratification
9. *Humane orientation*—encouraging fairness, altruism, friendliness, generosity, caring, and being kind to others.

The observation and study of the nine cultural dimensions validated by GLOBE is an incredible journey that definitely will assist us in addressing and understanding issues in all societies. Furthermore, a deep observation and study of the cultural dimensions will cause us to see the key role culture plays in the practice of leadership and how it is viewed and perceived by different societies around the world. Despite the fact that the GLOBE nine core cultural dimensions have remarkable significance in the study of culture and leadership, any leadership study is not complete without observing the cultural dimensions and their interactions.

I have chosen to focus on my observations and research on *individualism versus collectivism,* previously explained as the relationship between the individual and collectivity, or as explained by other scholars, the measure of the power of the individual or the group. So let's look at them closely.

## *Individualism vs. Collectivism*

The observation and study of individualism and collectivism is receiving a great deal of attention in the twentieth century. As the researchers of the GLOBE study pointed out, there are hundreds of published articles about these cultural dimensions. Many books have been exclusively dedicated to this topic, yet these are not new findings in the study of cultural dimensions. Have you ever wondered why in some countries individual goals take precedence over group goals? Or have you wondered why in some countries the pace of life is slower while in others countries it is faster? Let's observe these cultural dimensions more closely.

Individualism and collectivism have been exhibited in legal and religious institutions for thousands of years. Ancient civilizations protected the rights and safety of groups over that of individuals. In other words, the behavior of individuals was standardized to protect the group.

As explained by Hosftede (1994), the relation between the individual and collectivity is not only a matter of living together; it is also associated with societal norms. The individual act of converting to a new set of norms in an individualistic society could not generate changes in an individual's closest relatives, while if someone is converting to a new set of norms in a collectivist society, it is more likely that this conversion will take place with that person's closest relatives as well. As an example, Hosftede (1994) illustrated that the conversion of greater religions, as history has shown, is collective. In Acts 16:31, the apostle Paul explained to the Philippian jailer that to be saved, "Believe in the Lord Jesus, and you will be saved—you and your household." The jailer took Paul to his house so Paul could baptize him and his family. Another illustration by Hosftede (1994) on conversion that takes place with closer relatives is ideological conversions. Modern China, as stated by Hosftede, is one of the countries that exhibits this tendency, as ideological beliefs are part of family connections.

Even though there are many sources and much research to observe these cultural dimensions, the data and conclusions exposed by the GLOBE study are worthy to observe as there are no other studies that have its scope and depth (sixty-two nations at societal and organizational levels and multiple dimensions of leadership). The following tables summarize parallel individualism and collectivism characteristics and behaviors for societies (GLOBE), organizations (GLOBE), schools, and workplaces and in leadership (GLOBE), allowing us to increase our understanding and level of awareness and self-awareness on how these two cultural dimensions that basically explain the nature of the relationship between the individual and the group play a role in societies and organizations (such as schools and workplaces) and as a result it has a direct influence on leadership.

Higher Individualism-Collectivism Societies versus Lower
Individualism-Collectivism Societies

| Features of Cultures Thant Scores High on Collectivism | Features of Cultures That Score High on Individualism |
|---|---|
| • Individuals are integrated into strong cohesive groups<br>• The self is viewed as interdependent with groups<br>• Group goals take precedence over individual goals<br>• Duties and obligations are important determinants of social behavior<br>• People emphasize relatedness with groups<br>• Ecologies are agriculture, and countries are often developing<br>• There is a slower pace of life<br>• There are lower heart-attack rates<br>• There is lower subjective well-being<br>• There are more extended family structures<br>• Love is assigned less weight in marriage decisions<br>• There are lower divorce rates<br>• Communication is indirect<br>• Individuals are likely to engage in group activities | • Individuals look after themselves or their immediate families<br>• The self is viewed as autonomous and independent of groups<br>• Individual goals take precedence over group goals<br>• Attitudes and personal needs are important determinants of behavior<br>• People emphasize rationality<br>• Ecologies are hunting and gathering, or industrial and wealthy<br>• There is a faster pace of life<br>• There are higher heart-attack rates<br>• There is higher subjective well-being<br>• There are more nuclear family structures<br>• Love is assigned greater weight in marriage decisions<br>• There are higher divorce rates<br>• Communications is direct |

| | |
|---|---|
| • Individuals have fewer social interactions, but interactions tend to be longer and more intimate<br>• Individuals make greater distinctions between in-groups and out-groups | • Individuals are likely to engage in activities alone<br>• Individuals have more social interactions, but interactions tend to be shorter and less intimate<br>• Individuals make fewer distinctions between in-groups and out-groups |

Note: Although this table presents two extremes, it is important to recognize that these constructs represent a continuum and that, furthermore, there is also within-culture variation.

Higher Individualism and Collectivism for Organizations versus Lower Individualism and Collectivism for Organizations

| Organizations that Score High in Collectivism | Organizations that Score High in Individualism |
|---|---|
| • Members assume that they are highly interdependent with the organization and believe it is important to make personal sacrifices to fulfill their organizational obligations<br>• Employees tend to develop long-term relationship with employers from recruitment to retirement<br>• Organizations take responsibility for employee welfare | • Members assume that they are interdependent of the organization and believe it is important to bring their unique skills and abilities to the organization<br>• Employees develop short-term relationships, and change companies at their own discretion<br>• Organizations are primarily interested in the work that employees perform and not their personal or family welfare |

| | |
|---|---|
| • Important decisions tend to be made by groups | • Important decisions tend to be made by individuals |
| • Selection can focus on relational attributes of employees | • Selection focuses primarily on employees' knowledge, skills, and abilities |
| • Jobs are designed in groups to maximize the social and technical aspects of the job | • Jobs are designed individually to maximize autonomy |
| • Training is emphasized more than selection | • Selection is emphasized more than training |
| • Compensation and promotions are based on what is equitable for the group and on considerations of seniority and personal needs | • Compensation and promotions are based on an equity model, in which an individual is rewarded in direct relationship to his her contribution to task success |
| • Motivation is socially oriented, and is based on the need to fulfill duties and obligations and to contribute to the group | • Motivation is individually oriented, and is based on individual interest, needs, and capacities |
| • Organizational commitment is based on expectations of loyalty and in-group attitudes | • Organizational commitment is based on individuals' rational calculations of costs and benefits |
| • Prosocial behaviors, or organizational citizenship behaviors, are more common | • Prosocial behaviors, or organizational citizenship behaviors, are less common |
| • Avoidant, obliging, compromising, and accommodating conflict resolution tactics are preferred | • Direct and solution-oriented conflict resolution tactics are preferred |
| • Accountability for organizational successes and failures rests with groups | • Accountability for organizational successes and failures rests with individuals |

Implications of Individualism and Collectivism for Leadership

| In Collectivistic Cultures | In Individualistic Cultures |
|---|---|
| • Task-performance (P) leadership behaviors are perceived as being intimately related to relationship-maintenance (M) behaviors<br>• Leadership behaviors associated with task functions (P) tend to focus on relational interactions and behaviors associated<br>• Effective leaders are paternalistic and nurturant<br>• Leader behaviors emphasize group maintenance activities and face saving<br>• Leaders prototypes reflect cultural values of interdependence, collaborations, and self-effacement<br>• Charismatic leadership is highly valued | • Performance and maintenance behaviors are seen as more distinct<br>• Leadership behaviors associated with relational functions (M) tend to focus more on the task than in group-maintenance<br>• Effective leaders are less directive and more autonomous<br>• Leader behaviors emphasize individual discretion and task accomplishments<br>• Leaders prototypes reflect cultural values of being independent, strong willed, and forceful<br>• Charismatic leadership is less valued |

In general, we observe that individualism and collectivism have many implications for societies and organizations, such as schools and workplaces. It is important to observe how motivation and commitment have a significant role for both groups yet is achieved in different ways. As a result we can undoubtedly affirm that leadership effectiveness can vary in different cultures.

It is interesting to observe how cultural dimensions interact in different societies and organizations. Another important study, Hofstede in 1980, surveyed IBM employees from forty countries, uncovering five cultural dimensions, one of which was *individualism.* He found that most east Asian countries, including China, were *collectivist,* and the United States was *individualistic.* Collectivism has received much attention in this century, yet it manifested in cultural institutions thousands of years ago (House et al., 2004). As described by House and his colleagues, collectivism has numerous implications for organizations, including the nature of human resource management practices, motivation, job attitudes, group processes, organizational trust, accountability, and entrepreneurship. Furthermore, collectivist society management is described as the management of groups (Hofstede, 2001). For instance, the GLOBE ten-year study of sixty-two societies included 158 middle managers in mainland China (House et al., 2004). As explained by Mansour and Nandani in 2005, the GLOBE study estimated that over the next fifteen years, Chinese leaders would be influenced in their development by four tensions: empowerment versus autocracy, diversity versus insularity, self-sufficiency versus reliance on government, and global perspective versus national pride.

Many important studies on cultural dimensions have established how cultural changes impact leadership behaviors (House et al., 2004). For instance, a conceptual article by Jung, Bass, and Sosik in 1995 addressed the relationship between transformational leadership and collectivistic cultures. They suggest that the characteristics of transformational leadership are linked to collectivism and that transformational leadership processes are most likely to be enhanced in collectivistic cultures. In addition, they acknowledged that little research effort has been focused upon the linkage between transformational leadership and collectivistic cultures. To illustrate this point, Avolio and Bass in 2004 stated, "The mutual obligation in collectivist societies between leaders and followers facilitates the transformational leader's *individualized consideration*" (p. 41).

## *Cross-Cultural Leadership*

As previously explained, adding a cross-cultural constituent to the mix of leadership study makes the entire process more complex. Without a realistic setting to facilitate the narrowing and guiding of cross-cultural leadership research, there would be little lucidity to the research being performed (Deng & Gibson, 2008). However, as explained by House et al. in 2004, "the need for a better understanding of cultural influences on organizational practices and leadership has never been greater" (p. 10) because of increasing globalization and the economic codependence among nations. Leaders' influence, prestige, and privileges diverge extensively by culture, resulting in numerous challenges for organizations and leaders in multinational corporations. House et al. in 2004 stressed that these challenges include the identification and selection of appropriate leaders according to the culture in which they function; the design of multinational organizational structures; management of culturally diverse employees; and negotiations, sales, acquisitions, and mergers with organizations in other nations.

Cross-cultural research on leadership and organizations is helping us to test our knowledge, identify boundaries, recognize universal aspects of leadership, and more importantly, be able to adapt and work together. On this point there is agreement that understanding culture can open up new opportunities for leaders as culture plays a key role in the practice of leadership and how it is viewed. Certainly this includes recognizing that there are two important facets of culture in the context of leadership: the external environment of an organization interacts with and the internal culture or work environment (Dr. Glenn Williams, Outwardlooking.com, Feb. 2013). In most recent research, the ability to work effectively across cultures has been highlighted as cultural intelligence or cultural quotient (CQ). The researchers Livermore, Van Dyne, and Ang affirmed that intercultural capability as a form of intelligence can be measured and developed across cultures. They further stated that understanding the impact of the individual's cultural background and increasing the ability to adapt and interact with others from different cultures is essential in business effectiveness. Recent studies on this topic provide details on how CQ is seen as playing a more important role in success not only in the business arena but further in military and government strategies and operations.

As clarified by House et al. in 1997, leaders facing these challenges do not have enough guidance from the literature. There are undeniable reasons to understand the role of societal and organizational culture on leadership. What works effectively in one culture may not work in another culture (House et al., 2004; Laurent, 1983; Trompenaars, 1993). "Cross-cultural research and the development of cross-cultural theory are needed to fill this knowledge gap" (House et al., 2004, p. 10).

In Dorfman and Howell's 1997 study of managerial leadership in the United States and Mexico, a blend of directive and supportive leadership was found to be extremely effectual in Mexico. Such an extremely directive leadership style that also emphasizes status orientation, support, and involvement is usually referred to as a "paternalistic" style of leadership, a mode that is widespread in many developing countries (Dorfman & Howell, 1988, 1997; Kanungo & Mendonça, 1996).

Leadership in developing nations is high on power distance, with robust family bonds and a sense of fatalism (House et al., 2004). Furthermore, workers expect organizations and leaders to take care of them as well as their families (Pellegrini & Scandura, 2008). To further examine these suppositions, Jung and Avolio in 1999 evaluated transactional and transformational leadership styles. For individual and group-task conditions the end products were compared, and whether a different impact on individualists and collectivists carrying out brainstorming tasks could be found was evaluated. This study found that collectivist groups generate more ideas with a transformational leader, while the individualists produced additional ideas with a transactional leader. In another research investigation, collectivism was connected to the level of charismatic leadership, which in turn was assertively linked to supervisory ratings of job satisfaction, work-unit performance, leader effectiveness, and satisfaction with the leader (Pillai and Meindl, 1998, p. 647). Additionally, collectivism was statistically associated with affective facets of an individual's motivation to lead (Chan & Drasgow, 2001).

An illustration of an archetypal two-country appraisal comes from a 1999 research study by Kuchinke, contrasting US and German managers, engineers, and production employees of a telecommunications firm on the cultural work values and transformational and transactional leadership. In this exploration, US employees valued considerably higher levels of *charisma* and *inspirational motivation* in comparison to the German workers; no considerable differences were found for the other transformational and transactional procedures. Cultural work values also varied, with US employees ranking higher in individualism and masculinity but lower in long-term orientation. Additionally, masculinity, long-term orientation, and individualism notably forecast the two leadership styles of charisma and inspirational motivation, accounting for 7 percent of the variance in each leadership quality (Kuchinke, 1999, p. 143).

Ardichvili and Kuchinke in 2002 assessed leadership patterns across several cultures. In their research, transformational leadership and work cultural values were evaluated in a sample of large groups of managers and workers in the post-Communist and former USSR countries of Russia, Georgia, Kazakhstan, and Kyrgystan. Geletkanycz's 1997 research focused on how commitment to the status quo is shaped by personal values and national cultures by collecting survey data on leadership and corporate strategy from 1,540 top managers in a wide assortment of firms in twenty nations (Geletkanycz, 1997, p. 8). His research revealed that the commitment to the status quo quotient was strongest among executives in national locations that stress individual over collective action and focus on the short-term over the long. In addition, differences remained even among executives with broad careers in the industry, implying that national cultures have a consistent impact on managerial behavior.

Effective leader behaviors have also been revealed in other studies, such as research of US and European managers conducted by Robie, Johnson, Nilsen, and Hazucha in 2001. They found that managerial skills, such as the "drive for results" and "analyzing issues" approaches, are universally effective leader behaviors, and these two skills were the best forecasters of managerial performance as rated by supervisors. Leslie and Van Velsor in 1998 found that US and European managers distinguish effective leaders as those giving value to personal influence, collaboration, and recognition of rules and procedures laid down by an external authority.

Pfeifer and Love in 2004 investigated the leadership qualities of New Zealand's two largest cultural groups, the *Māori* and *Pakeha*. Their study examined the degree to which these leadership features were entrenched in the distinctive milieus of each culture. Followers' opinions of leadership behavior were inspected employing the Multifactor Leadership Questionnaire (MLQ). The hypothesis that leadership is profoundly embedded in the broader cultural contexts was supported, yielding cautious confirmation that leadership ideas are culturally sanctioned in New Zealand. These findings, if validated by additional and more exhaustive research, would establish the vital necessity for public communicators to search for ways to propagate information to these groups, particularly when working through opinion leaders.

The 2002 comparative study of countries by Ardichvili and Kuchinke highlighted the full spectrum of the leadership framework, which contrasted leadership styles and ethnic values for over four thousand managerial and non-managerial employees in ten business organizations in Georgia, Russia, Germany, Kazakhstan, Kyrgyzstan, and the United States. For sociocultural dimensions, the survey revealed that in comparison to Germany and the United States, the four former USSR nations varied principally in higher levels of *masculinity,* much lower levels of *power distance,* and much longer planning horizons. The outcomes on leadership designate that two dimensions—*contingent reward* and *inspirational motivation*—generated the highest scores in all four countries of the former USSR. Two less-efficacious leadership styles, *laissez-faire* and *management by exception,* got considerably higher scores in the four former USSR nations than in the United States and Germany. Finally, the study implied that cross-cultural human resource development concerns cannot be depicted by simplified dichotomies between the East and the West.

Prior literature documented the incredible diversity of organizations' practices around the world. From the 2003 research of Davis and Bryant, working in groups or alone is viewed differently around the world, influencing the efficacy of virtual teams in multinational organizations. Brodbeck et al. in 2000 explained the management dilemma in the European Union, where management practices used to stop at national boundaries.

The previous research and findings increased my interest in understanding how the attributes of transformational leadership and the values of collectivistic societies relate. Furthermore, it increased my interest in how cultural behaviors and beliefs are affected or change when we are interacting in a different culture. We'll observe how these elements relate in more depth by examining acculturation.

## Acculturation

It is impossible to deny the cultural clashes and incredible cultural phenomena that take place in the process of acculturation from one society to another. This phenomenon takes on a great and complex scale when the process of acculturation takes place from a collective society to an individualist society or vice versa. In most cases emigrants from one country to another faced an emotional limbo, a period of time when they were in that midpoint, the halfway home that didn't let them settle in this country yet at the same time didn't let them go back to their native country. After a while, some emigrants are comfortable with the acculturation level that they reach, while some don't acculturate to the new society. The uncertainty previously referred to as an emotional limbo is faced by thousand of emigrants through their acculturation process. Some emigrants might take more years than others to reach a point of comfort in their acculturation process, and the outcome might vary as well. Some emigrants will separate from their countries and native cultures, assimilating into the culture around them to become a part of the "melting pot" as is widely stressed in US society; others will connect with their own ethnic groups, maintaining the language and cultures and becoming a part of the "cultural mosaic" greatly stressed in Canadian society.

There is a fair amount of research on the topics of emotional acculturation, the melting pot, and cultural mosaic, all undoubtedly great topics for analysis on their implications on leadership. As a matter of fact, we cannot ignore their impact on the way all of us lead. Culture's worldview remains in the background, as instinctively we carry with us an enormous range of assumptions about what is visible or invisible, about time and cause and effect, and about values.

In general, the process that can occur when two or more cultures interact together is called acculturation (Suinn et al., 1992). The possible outcomes of acculturation include assimilation, whereby a host culture absorbs the immigrant culture, and multiculturalism, whereby both cultures exist side by side. At the individual level, as explained by Suinn et al. in 1992, "exposure to another culture can lead a person to resisting change in his/her values and behavioral competencies, adopting the host culture's values and behavioral skills and styles as a replacement for his/her parent culture's values/ behaviors, acquiring host culture values/behaviors while retaining parent culture values/behaviors with situational reliance determining which values/behaviors are in effect at different times" (p. 4).

Acculturation is a phenomenon resulting from groups of individuals having different cultures who come into constant personal contact, producing changes in the original culture patterns of either or both groups. Acculturation comprises the learning and adoption of values and norms of the adopted society. Newcomers with the same cultural and ethnic backgrounds will experience acculturation, yet the outcomes may be different.

Suinn et al. in 1992 further stressed that the identity of an individual involves self-perception or subjective statement of his/her cultural character; therefore, identity is declared by the individual. Hence, it is possible that a person's self-definition might be in contrast to the actual behavioral competencies or values possessed or expressed by the individual. For example, an individual might fully possess the behavioral competencies essential to fit and be accepted into a Western atmosphere (job, school, residence, etc.), yet privately this individual may retain the identity of being Asian (Suinn et al., 1992). Berry in 1980 suggested four basic stages of acculturation: integration, assimilation, separation/segregation, and marginalization.

Other studies have found that acculturation is a multidimensional process. For instance, Gordon in 1964 identified seven dimensions of the acculturation/assimilation process: cultural assimilation (acculturation), structural assimilation, marital assimilation, identificational assimilation, attitude receptional assimilation, behavior receptional assimilation, and civic assimilation. This model of acculturation denotes that acculturation is a process in which an individual begins with cultural assimilation (acculturation) and ends with complete assimilation that is characterized by the absence of conflict between value and power with the host society (Hazuda, Stern, & Haffner, 1988, p. 690).

Acculturation is now widely accepted as being orthogonal rather than linear. For example, Oetting and Beauvais posited in 1991 that it is possible for an individual to have a high identification with culture X and low identification with culture Z, or low identification with culture X and high identification with culture Z, or high identification with both or low identification with both.

LaFromboise, Coleman, and Gerton in 1993 suggested a five-model orthogonal acculturation framework, with the five patterns of assimilation, acculturation, alternation, multicultural, and fusion. Each pattern is rated on the emphasis it places on seven process variables related to second-culture acquisition: contact with culture of origin, loyalty to culture of origin, involvement with culture of origin, acceptance by members of culture of origin, contact with the second culture, affiliation with the second culture, and acceptance by members of the second culture.

Acculturation can diverge according to the ethnic of the immigrant group and the host group. Besides, there are many factors such as different cultures, languages, and immigration histories that influence acculturation-related outcomes.

The Hispanic culture lately is having a big wave in United States as the Hispanic population had a big presence in the last presidential elections. Some sources stated that President Barack Obama won reelection due in part to near-record levels of support from Latino voters (CNN, 2012). Further, marketing statistics experts stated that the Hispanic population is projected to nearly triple from 2008 to 2050; thus nearly one in three US residents would be Hispanic. As "Hispanos" are a rapidly evolving, the assimilation and acculturation processes are intensely studied for this group. This is definitely a great topic for a future study, as the Hispanic population is basically a collective society. Researchers believe that Hispanics do not assimilate but instead acculturate without letting go of customs and/or language (Malaghan, 2012), a topic worthy of research and understanding in the near future.

A number of acculturation scales instruments have been developed to assess specific ethnic groups, such as Asian Americans—the Suinn-Lew Asian Self-Identity Acculturation Scale, or SL-ASIA (Suinn et al., 1992); and Chinese Americans—the General Ethnic Questionnaire-Chinese version (Tsai et al, 2000). The SL-ASIA scale originally consisted of twenty-one multiple-choice questions that covered: language, identity, friendship choice, behaviors, generation/

geographic history, and attitudes. In the most recent version, questions twenty-one to twenty-six were added to further classify participants in ways that use current theorizing multidimensional and orthogonal and not linear or unidimensional (Suinn et al., 1992). The SL-ASIA has been applied to Asian groups such as Vietnamese Americans (Duan & Vu, 2000), Chinese Americans (Tata & Leong, 1994), and Japanese Americans (Atkinson & Matsushita, 1991) based on samples composed of college students. Further, the use of one scale for all Asian groups may not reflect the cultural qualities of a specific group (Suinn et al., 1987), such as the Chinese. According to the authors, it appears that a different scale for each specific Asian group is more appropriate in the same way as is necessary to design separate instruments for Hispanic groups such as Mexicans and Cubans. Moreover, Duan and Vu stated in 2000 that the scale fails to identify situational behaviors, and this limitation is particularly significant since situational behavior is a characteristic of Chinese culture.

Chinese immigrants experience multiple difficulties when they arrive and try to adjust to life in the United States. However, many of them attain social and financial success not only within their ethnic communities but in American social environments as well (Mizokawa & Ryckman, 1990; Sue & Okazaki, 1990). Chinese immigrants carry cultural values that emphasize high resilience, such as *collectivism,* or the inclination to prioritize group needs over individual needs (Hofstede, 1980); *relational orientation,* where the self is defined through continuous interdependence with others (Yee, Debaryshe, Yuen, Kim, & McCubbin, 1998); and *family obligation,* where the younger generation is expected to demonstrate respect, obedience, and continual care of the children and elders' well-being (Chao & Tseng, 2002; Xu, Xie, Liu, Xia, & Liu, 2007). These values, endorsed by older Chinese generations, are the significant factor of resilience in Chinese immigrants (Yeh, Kim, Pituc, & Atkins, 2008). New Chinese immigrants face the pressure to acculturate into the Western culture in order to survive; they encounter major changes in communication, social support network, and roles within their families, jobs, and education (Zhou, 1997). Even first-generation immigrants can be exposed to American European values from interaction with college peers and the general academia setting (Biesta, 2007). Research regarding Chinese immigrants' resiliency has suggested that first-generation immigrants demonstrate highly resilient behaviors in a foreign country because of the traditional "hard work and effort equals success" value that is essential and central in Chinese cultures (Plucker, 1994; Siu & Shek, 2005).

# 3

## Transformational Leadership and Collectivism Societies

In the late 1990s, transactional leadership theory was the most studied method of leadership theory (Avolio, Walderman, & Yanimarina, 1991; Seltzer & Bass, 1990). Transactional leadership theory focuses on the interactions between leaders and followers (Burns, 1978; Heifetz, 1994). These interactions allow leaders to gain influence and sustain it over time. It is a process based on reciprocity, wherein the leader earns influence by adjusting to the expectations of followers and at the same time is under followers' influence (Stone & Patterson, 2005).

This leadership method, in which leaders exchange rewards for employees' compliance, is a concept based on bureaucratic authority and a leader's legitimacy in an organization (Tracey & Hinkin, 1994; Yukl, 2002). The reward exchange includes the leader's ability to fulfill promises of recognition, advancement for employees who perform well, and pay increases (Bass, 1990). Essentially, transactional leaders employ rewards as their most important source of power. Followers abide by the lead of the leader when the exchange meets followers' needs. Such relationships persist as long as the incentive or reward is desired by the follower and both the leader and the follower view the agreement as a means of advancing toward their personal goals (Bass, 1990).

Transactional leaders give confidence to followers by clarifying the roles and requirements needed (Management by Exception–active/passive) to meet their goals and offering recognition when goals are achieved (Contingent Reward). In depth, management by exception-active is characterized by leaders who focus, deal, and keep track of mistakes, exceptions, deviations, and irregularities from standards and take quick actions to correct them; management by exception-passive fails to interfere or take action until the problem becomes serious or procedures are not met. Transactional contingent reward provides assistance, clarifies responsibility and expectations in exchange for the effort to achieve targets, and finally expresses satisfaction when expectations are met (Avolio, Bass, Walumbwa, & Zhu, 2004).

The limitations for the transactional approach, as explained by Avolio et al. in 2004, are that it first includes managers under-using methods because of time pressures, poor appraisal methods, doubts about the efficacy of positive reinforcement, and discomfort of leaders and associates. Second, transactional leaders embrace those who do not have the reputation and resources needed to deliver promised rewards. Finally, limitations take account of the fact that a noncontingent reward sometimes works as well as a contingent reward to reinforce performance, rendering the transactional approach unnecessary.

Thus, transformational leadership becomes the new paradigm adding to the transactional leadership model. As explained by Waldman and Bass in 1986, Howell and Avolio in 1993, and Waldman, Bass, and Yammarino in 1990, transformational leadership does not replace transactional leadership; in fact, transformational leaders can be transactional when suitable. Bass suggested in 1985 that transformational leadership augments transactional leadership in achieving the goals of the leader, associate, group, and organization.

According to Van Seters and Field in 1993, the latest and most promising phase of leadership theory is transformational leadership. Bass and Avolio described transformational leadership in 1994 as "an expansion of transactional leadership" (p. 3). Van Seters and Field inferred in 1993 that the dramatic improvement of transformational leadership over all previous theories is that it is based on intrinsic rather than extrinsic motivation. The leaders must be proactive rather than reactive in their thinking, radical rather than conservative, open to new ideas, and more creative and innovative (Bass, 1995). Transformational leadership is useful and valuable in producing and maintaining organizational changes.

As the definition implies, transformational leadership goes beyond focusing on the exchange between leaders and followers to a more extensive standpoint, raising the interests of employees, inspiring workers to look further than their own interests to what would benefit the group, and cheering employees to acknowledge the organization's undertakings as their own (Sanders, Hopkins, & Geroy, 2003). Since its emergence, transformational leadership has received significant attention. In the late 1970s and the 1980s, researchers identified many of the attributes of an effective transformational leader. Studies from Bass in 1985, Bennis and Nanus in 1985, Tichy and Devanna in 1986, Conger and Kanungo in 1987, Kouzes and Posner in 1987, and House and Ram in 1997 suggested there are universal attributes of transformational leaders. Bass argued in 1997 that charisma, intellectual stimulation of followers, and individualized consideration toward followers are near-universal components of transformational leadership. Furthermore, House et al. conveyed in 2004 that those universal characteristics are considered effective across cultures.

## *Factors of Transformational Leadership*

Transformational leaders may use numerous techniques in accomplishing their objectives, such as stimulating employees using the power of charisma exclusively, appealing to an employee's emotional needs, or stimulating employees intellectually (Sanders et al., 2003). As affirmed by Burns in 1978, transformational leaders ask followers to surpass their own self-interest for the good of the group, organization, or society; to consider their long-term needs to develop themselves, rather than addressing their immediate needs; and to become more aware of what is really important. Thus, through this interaction, followers are converted into leaders. Associates' confidence levels rise, and their needs broaden from leadership that encourages growth to a higher potential. This special motivation is linked to empirically derived factors of transformational leadership: idealized influence (behaviors and attributes), inspirational motivation, intellectual stimulation, and individualized consideration (Bass, 1985).

## *Idealized Influence*

Associates view these leaders in an idealized way. They are admired, trusted, and respected. Followers' needs are considered first and above leaders' needs. The risk is shared and leaders are consistent in conducting their mission with essential ethics, values, and principles (Avolio et al., 2004).

## *Inspirational Motivation*

Motivation is built in for followers by providing meaning and challenge to their work. The leader stimulates team spirit as well as instilling followers with optimism and enthusiasm about the future.

The leader also articulates confidence about the achievement of goals and a clear vision (Avolio et al., 2004).

## *Intellectual Stimulation*

The followers' efforts to be innovative and creative are stimulated by approaching old situations in a new way, questioning, and reframing problems. Thus, new ideas and creative solutions to problems are constructed through teamwork. There is no criticism in public for mistakes. Problems are observed from another angle to provide new ways to complete assignments (Avolio et al., 2004).

## *Individual Consideration*

Leaders act as coaches or mentors to each follower. Learning opportunities are created so there is room to grow. Each follower is considered different from others and not just as a member of a group. Thus, each follower develops to higher levels of potential (Avolio et al., 2004).

## *Transformational Leadership Studies and Research*

During the last two decades, there has been a significant increase in testing transactional and transformational leadership, including many theses and doctoral dissertations on the topic (Avolio, 1999; Bass, 1998; Bass & Avolio, 1994). The most commonly employed measure of transformational and transactional leadership is the Multifactor Leadership Questionnaire (MLQ), developed by B. Bass in 1985. The MLQ's most recent version, 5X, has been designed to test a broader range of leadership behaviors, focusing on individual behaviors. The MLQ-5X tests leadership styles from laissez-faire to charismatic leadership, expanding the leadership styles (Avolio et al., 2004). The MLQ has been used in different cultures in the international context (Koh, Steers, & Terborg, 1995; Den Hartog, Van Muijen, & Koopman, 1997; Carless, 1998; Geyer & Steyrer, 1998). Bass suggested in 1998 that even though each cultural group is likely to attribute different characteristics to leadership behavior, some behavioral characteristics, specifically those associated with transformational leadership, are likely to be universally endorsed as contributing to outstanding leadership. Transactional and transformational leadership have been used to assess the perceptions of leadership effectiveness of executives, managers, supervisors, and team leaders from all levels of the organization and across different types of production, service, and military organizations (Avolio et al., 2004).

Transformational leadership has been studied extensively. For example, Frey's 2007 study on personality attributes and transformational leadership in different levels of managers includes measurements from Basic Adlerian Scales for Interpersonal Success—Adult Form (BASIS-A), the Hogan Personality Inventory (HPI), and MLQ-5X. The study demonstrated that the striving for perfection and wanting recognition scales from the BASIS-A as well as the ambition scale from the HPI were predictive of participants who demonstrated a transformational style of leadership.

In a 2008 study by Meredith on executives leading nonprofit, faith-based organizations in Colorado, the United States compared transformational, transactional, and laissez-faire leadership styles with scores on the Baron Emotional Quotient Inventory Test (EQ-i). Statistical cluster analysis demonstrated a strong relationship between transformational leadership and emotional intelligence. Furthermore, linear regression analysis revealed that five components of emotional intelligence accounted for over half of the variation in transformational leadership behavior (p. 72). This study suggests that developing emotional intelligence in executive leaders could increase the likelihood of the use of transformational leadership behaviors.

Research in a different cultural context recognized transformational leadership, as in Iwuh's 2010 study of the frequencies at which leaders at the Nigerian National Economic and Empowerment Development Strategy (NEEDS) exhibited transformational leadership characteristics at the Federal Ministry of National Planning Commission (NPC) in Abuja, Nigeria. This study showed that leaders exhibited a moderate level of transformational leadership characteristics. The results came from the leaders' and their subordinates' perceptions. Thus, the study recommended that NEEDS/NPC leaders acquire at least a moderate-high frequency of the characteristics of transformational leadership to guarantee accomplishing the United Nations Millennium Development Goal of cutting poverty in half in Nigeria by 2015.

One of the studies from the Great Lakes Institute of Management on transformational leadership concluded that employees in organizations are emotionally attached and have a sense of loyalty to the extent that they feel "obligated to say" when they perceive that supervisors demonstrate transformational leadership. Some researchers even extend the study to genders, explaining that female leaders are more transformational leaders than males. According to this meta-analytic review, women leaders engage more often in a reward-contingency behavior, while men are more likely to focus on followers' mistakes and managing problems as they occur; which is basically a transactional leadership style. Gender is definitely an important inference for this study, one I am sure will provide value to new generations.

In brief, studies and research on this topic, even if the number remains small, have wondered whether transformational leadership style is more appropriate to a collectivist society and transactional leadership style for an individualist society, further questioning if people prefer a leader who is more representative of their orientation. These questions remains unanswered, and more research on this topic is crucial as new generations globalize their world. Perhaps global leadership needs to be more transformational through the awareness of how cultural values highly influence its practice and outcome. There is no doubt that understanding of people's beliefs and values is crucial for today's globalized world and its deep battle for companies and organizations around the globe to be successful across borders.

# 4

## Synopsis of the Study

### *Introduction*

The research study investigates the relationship between acculturation and leadership style/practices of Chinese business leaders living and working in the United States. A limited quantitative and qualitative study in a two-phase sequential mixed method design was used integrating numerical data and text. The analysis was focused on the correlation between acculturation scores and demographics (independent variables) and leadership styles/practices (dependent variables). The quantitative method included two assessments: the SL-ASIA scale and the Multifactor Leadership Questionnaire 5X (MLQ-5X).

The findings of this study suggested that acculturation scores have a significant correlation with leadership style/practices; further, that a relationship exists between acculturation scores determined by the Suinn-Lew Asian Self Identity Acculturation scale (SL-ASIA) and the leadership style/practices of the business leaders as defined by the Multifactor Leadership Questionnaire (MLQ-5X).

## *Significance of the Study*

In general, this research study may promote an exclusive discussion among Chinese, American, Chinese-American and international business leaders. This discussion aims at the relationship and understanding of multinational business leaders in managing multicultural employees transcending cultural perspectives. Also, this research study ambition identifies specific acculturation and leadership variables from Chinese business leaders living and working in the United States. The most leadership studies focused on data obtained from study participants and researchers are from the United States (Pedersen & Connerley, 2005). Therefore, as cultural diversity increases it is significant that studies are wide-ranging their selection of samples (Magala, 2005).

## *Significance of the Study Contribution*

As the understanding of Chinese business leaders is vital to the American and global economy, this study may facilitate the comprehension of their leadership evolution and current leadership style/practice. Thus, the findings of this study may have added to the body of knowledge on cross-cultural leadership.

The findings of this study may help American business leaders who presently live and work in the United States understand the Chinese business leader's current leadership style/practice and how Chinese business leaders are culturally influenced in the United States. In this fashion, this study may add to training programs aimed to lower cultural barriers in negotiations and in the workplace.

## *Significance of the Study to Leadership*

The findings and conclusions of this study will contribute both theoretically and empirically to the: cross-culture leadership literature, acculturation, American leadership, Chinese leadership, Chinese business leaders, and transactional and transformational leadership theories. The art of leading in a global context, as discussed by Mendenhall (2006) is a cultural, sense-making endeavor. Hence, leadership researches highlight that cross-cultural studies increase as the world globalized (Pedersen & Connerley, 2005). As a result, this study may stimulate further studies on cultural influence on leadership styles in cross-cultural environments.

Additionally, this study is significant due to its practical perspective. China's fast and remarkable evolution of its economy is not only attracting many non-Chinese businesses to set up new business operations in mainland China, but also many Chinese business leaders are setting up new businesses in other parts of the world, including the United States. Therefore, the knowledge and understanding of Chinese business leaders and their current leadership style may facilitate trust and confidence in business relations and negotiations.

## Chinese Leadership

Traditional and contemporary leadership in China are strongly connected. It is evident that leadership in China has been influenced by different leadership styles from the rest of the world, yet Chinese traditional and contemporary leadership has been guided by Chinese philosophical and cultural principles and thoughts for centuries. Gallo (2008) assessed that the foundations of Chinese business leaders continue to have a strong influence on contemporary Chinese leaders and certainly on business leaders.

## Chinese Traditional and Contemporary Leadership

*Chinese traditional leadership.* As explained by Sheh (2002), the phenomenon of leadership cannot be studied without recognizing that "the charisma of a truly Chinese leader or ruler and the leadership strategies demonstrated today are not new; in fact, they have long existed in the great civilizations of China for the last 4,000 years (p. 79). To understand Chinese leaders is vital to reviewing the philosophies of China's leadership, from the benevolent leadership of Confucius, the legalistic leadership of Han Fei Zi, the naturalistic leadership uncovered by Lao Zi, to the strategic leadership expounded by Sun Zi (Sheh, 2002).

*Confucius.* Born around 551 B.C., Confucius died at the age of 73 in 479 B.C. According to Chinese tradition, a thinker, political figure, educator, and founder of the Ru School of Chinese Thought, a legacy that is preserved in the *Lunyu* or *Analects* (Stanford Encyclopedia of Philosophy, 2006). Confucius illustrated the concepts of leadership from two points of view: social ethical values and individual ethical values. Presuming that individual values were practically associated with leadership, social values are indivisible from organizational culture because culture is essentially a mixture of values and practices in organizations or society (Swidler, 1986). For Confucius, both ethical values as fundamental factors to attaining ideal leadership and a harmonious social order are indissoluble relations between leadership and organizational culture. In brief, Confucius saw the leader or ruler as a moral manager possessing cultural leadership. Confucius also viewed the ruler as a gentleman, a man of compassion, good judgment, and courage. For Confucius, these were vital requisites for a ruler to possess to be a moral manager in a collectivist society (Bond & Hwang, 1986).

According to Oh (1991), Confucianism at present describes the accurate and truthful observance of human bonds in a hierarchically oriented society. Specifically, emphasis is given to the five constant virtues and corresponding cardinal relationships: filial piety, faithfulness, brotherhood, loyalty, and sincerity. Confucius' *Five Cardinal Relations*, that is, between sovereign and subject, father and son, elder brother and younger brother, husband and wife, and between friends, stipulated clear-cut relations between superiors and subordinates. In such settings, everyone knows their place and to whom they must show deference; these status differences are considered to be the right way to carry out relationships that are generally acknowledged and sustained at all levels of the hierarchy (Bond, 1991; Hofstede & Bond, 1988).

Sheh (2002) stressed that Confucianism deeply influenced the lives and thoughts of the Chinese people, which extends to today. Furthermore, the GLOBE study, based on the strong historical influence of China and Confucian ideology on several societies, established the *Confucian Asia Cluster* that includes: Singapore, Hong Kong, Taiwan, China, South Korea, and Japan, to facilitate the analysis in variations of specific cultural and leadership dimensions (House et al., 2004). The Confucian influence extends not only to the societies located close to China, but also overseas where Chinese communities are located (Brett, 1997). Confucianism in China itself has provided the foundation for a system of education that is more than 2,000 years old.

*Han Fei Zi.* (Also Han Fei Tzu or Han Fei) Born 281 B.C. and died at the age of 48 in 233 B.C., Han Fei Zi was a Chinese philosopher who crystallized thoughts in some 55 essays, believing that people are naturally evil, needing severe rules and rigorous punishment. According to Han Fei Zi, harsh laws prevent crime or any kind of violation; thus, if punishment is severe enough, it will hardly need to be used again because few people will have the courage to break the law (Sheh, 2002). Thus, for the legalist "it is more important to keep the people from doing evil through strict laws than to encourage people doing good through moral persuasion" (p. 93). The legalist controls the state with the help of three concepts: the position of power (*Shi*), certain techniques (*Shu*), and laws (*Fa*), assuming that everyone acts to avoid punishment and simultaneously tries to achieve gains (Watson, 1964). Han Fei Zi stated that a country's strength depends on law and that the body of officials should be the ones who follow the discipline of laws and regulations. Han Fei Zi also believed that if something follows the law, it is good; if not, it is bad, and stated that men are equal according to the law regardless of their status on influence and that laws need to be reviewed and changed in order to reflect the changing environment (Creel, 1974; Liao, 1939).

*Lao Zi.* (Also Lao Tse, Lao Tu, Lao Tzu, Laotze) The dates of this philosopher's birth and death remain unknown. Lao Zi is believed to have lived between the sixth and fourth centuries B.C. Lao Zi's real name is unknown; in Chinese the meaning of "Lao Zi" is "the old guy." As a Chinese philosopher, Lao Zi was the founder of Taoism and, according to tradition, author of Tao Te Ching or Dao De Jing, a two-part book with 81 chapters and about 5,000 characters, one of the most influential philosophical thoughts in Chinese civilization. Tao Te Ching strongly influenced the schools of legalism, Confucianism, and Buddhism, and is known to have put forth the central thoughts of Chinese religion. Its influence is known outside East Asia and has been translated to Western languages (Sheh, 2002).

The central idea of Lao Zi was to live a simple life and learn to live simply, understand and accept life as it is, and believe in being natural (Ball, 2004). As further explained by Sheh (2002), Lao Zi's principles of opposites, fluidity, paradox, and holism help leaders to better understand their duties as leaders. In general, Lao Zi's principles show leaders the importance of choosing the middle path and practicing moderation as it is observed in organizational theory; to lead with no possession, bias, or coercion, and to serve the people from the lowest level, acting as a facilitator; to be able to execute plans without weakening interpersonal relationships, being able to attract, retain, and motivate good people in an organization; and to be able to see things in terms of its parts and their relationship to becoming team players (Sheh, 2002).

*Sun Zi.* (Also Sun Wu and Sun Tzu) Living between the sixth and fifth centuries B.C., Sun Zi was a Chinese military commander, strategist, and philosopher, author of the *Art of War*, a 13-chapter work. The *Art of War* has been described as one of the masterpieces of strategy.

Its popularity is especially great among business and management leaders and researchers. As explained by Michaelson (2001), "Although the original text is founded in military strategy, the applications in this book focus on strategic issues for managers" (p. xxi).

To effectively lead, Sun Tzu believed that a leader must display qualities of moral influence, strategy, and organizational structure (Sheh, 2002). Furthermore, the leader should have the intelligence and analytical abilities to develop and nurture the needed skills. The major skill designated by this capability is the capacity to discern the territory and be able to understand the tactics that provide the best opportunities (Gagliardi, 1999, 2001).

As Gagliardi, (2001) explained, Sun Tzu holds trustworthiness as a necessary attribute for a leader to be effective. In a unit, Sun Tzu believed that a leader must inspire men's devotion and that a follower should be confident and never fear danger or untruthfulness. In fact, Sun Tzu stressed that one could lead people to their death only if the leader first earned their trust and got the followers to share their leader's vision (Gagliardi, 2004). Sun Tzu recommended that a leader must care for the soldiers; the contemporary analogue to this is *extroversion* (Hartman, 1999). As described by Gagliardi (1999), Sun Tzu explained that "personality traits found to be especially relevant for leadership effectiveness include high energy and stress tolerance, self-confidence, internal locus of control, emotional maturity, personal integrity, socialized power, motivation and high achievement orientation" (p. 23).

Sun Tzu inferred that the leader should be courageous and as "military officers that are committed lose their fear" (Gagliardi, 1999, p. 123). The modern equivalent could be openness to experience. This personality trait is the key to employing feedback from subordinates to improve one's performance (Smither, London, & Richmond, 2005). Sun Tzu, as a military leader, likewise exalted the trait of *strictness/discipline* as vital:

> We must be willing to do the unpleasant parts of the job
> as well as the fun parts. We must honor our agreements
> scrupulously. People must be able to depend on us. If
> we are not reliable, no one will support us for long.
> (Gagliardi, 2004, p. 45)

## *Chinese Contemporary Leadership*

China has undergone numerous wars that led to the strengthening of national consciousness about values of collective efforts and identity protection. Following dictates of leading philosophical and moral teachings, the Chinese people have learned to establish a system wherein there is safety in coming together to pool resources and efforts (Wakeman & Wakeman, 2009). Revolutions like Mao Zedong have emphasized cultural adherence and the maintenance of Chinese nationalism and identity. For instance, one of the famous quotes from Mao Zedong (1966) was that "the unification of our country, the unity of our people and the unity of our various nationalities—these are the basic guarantees of the sure triumph of our cause" (p. 2).

Chinese politics and governance have undergone many changes since the nation declared its independence as the People's Republic of China on October 1, 1949 (Shi, 2000). Mao Zedong offered China a new government approach to ensure that the communist party would maintain its dictatorial regime. Then Deng Xiaoping, General Secretary of the Communist Party from 1956 to 1967 and Paramount Leader from 1978 to the early 1990s, a reformer who led China toward a market economy, stated that democracy was an important condition for emancipating the mind. Both leaders agreed that democracy is not a goal, it is a key element to reach "China's real purpose of becoming a country that could no longer be bullied by outside powers" (Shi, 2000, p. 2). Furthermore, Hu Jintao, President of the People's Republic of China since 2003, addressed the National People's Congress in 2007, saying, "Developing democracy and improving the legal system are basic requirements of the social system" (Shi, 2000, p. 3). In 2006 party leaders were elected through direct voting in 296 townships in 16 provinces; nevertheless, China is not a democracy. China has been known for its substantial incongruities. Its economy is capitalist, while its political regimen is communist (Kynge, 2006). As Thornton (2008) elucidated the use of the term *democracy* as a goal of the government, it differs from the Western ideal of democracy and has different meanings and implications for every Chinese leader. The monopoly of political power is held by the Chinese Communist Party (CCP) (Shambaugh, 1993); there is no freedom of speech and no autonomous judiciary (Thornton, 2008).

From the writings of Cheng (2001), five political generations are identified from contemporary Chinese history (Table 1). One of the focuses of Cheng's five-generation table is the *Primary Age Group by 1999*, which accentuates the fact that the new generation of leaders is young in comparison with the other generations—well-educated technocrats or professionals, mainly engineers. The youthful leaders in the fourth generation include: Paramount Leader or core figure, President Hu Jintao; Representative Wen Jiabao, the sixth and current Premier of the State Council, is the head of government and leads the cabinet; Zen Qinghong, Secretary of Secretariat of the Communist Party and member of the Politburo Standing Committee; Wu Bangguo, Chair of the Standing Committee; and Li Changchun, propaganda chief of the CCP and fifth-ranked member of the Politburo Standing Committee (Cheng, 2001).

Table 1

*Political Elite Generations in Communist China*

| Generation of leaders | Major historical event | Period of event | Paramount leader ("core figure") | Representative figures | Primary age group by 1999 |
|---|---|---|---|---|---|
| 1<sup>st</sup> generation | The Long March | 1934–1935 | Mao Zedong | Zhou Enlai Liu Shaoqi Lin Biao Den Xiaoping | Late 80s or older |
| 2<sup>nd</sup> generation | The Anti-Japanese War | 1937–1945 | Den Xiaoping | Hu Yaobang, Zhao Ziyang Hua Guofeng Qiao shi | Late 70s and 80s |
| 3<sup>rd</sup> generation | The Social Transformation | 1949–1958 | Jiang Zemin | Li Peng Zhu Rongji Li Lanqing Li Ruihuan | 60s and early 70s |
| 4<sup>th</sup> generation | The Cultural Revolution | 1966–1976 | Hu Jintao | Wen Jiabao Zeng Qinghong Wu Bangguo Li Changchun | Late 40s and 50s |
| 5<sup>th</sup> generation | The Economic Reform | 1978– | Unknown | Unknown | Early 40s |

From "China's Leaders a New Generation," by L. Cheng, 2001, 1, p. 9. Copyright © 2001 by Rowman and Littlefield Publishers, Inc.

Contemporary leadership in China has been shaped by major historical events as shown in Table 1, which sustain the categorization of the different generations of leaders. The first and second generations were recognized as the Republican Era (1911-1949), which was a period with a political instability that culminated in the Civil War (1945-1949), that ended with Mao

Zedong's Chinese Communist Party in power (Egri & Ralston, 2004). These periods also were recognized for extreme poverty and natural disasters (Vohra, 2000). During these periods, the cultural values were based on Confucianism emphasizing the virtues of propriety, benevolence, respect for social hierarchy, and commitment to collective interests was at the root of "Chineseness" (Xing 1995). Western ideas blended with Confucian ideology due to the presence of European and North American missionaries and trade relations (Xing, 1995).

The third generation was mainly recognized as a Consolidation Era (1950-1965). The Chinese Communist Party aimed to replace Confucianism with Maoist and Marxist-Leninist ideology (Ladany, 1988) to establish a new collective order that placed the State and the Communist Party beyond traditional individual and family concerns. Ties with the USSR grew; thus, Western presence in China was relegated to a negligible level (Egri & Ralston, 2004). Political consolidation brought greater economic and political stability, yet centralized industrialization and agrarian reform efforts were not effective (Yao, 2000). During the final part of the Consolidation Era (1961-1965), the rising influence of a moderate leadership style of Deng Xiaoping triggered a fractional conflict (Vohra, 2000).

The major historical event that shaped the fourth generation of leaders is the Great Cultural Revolution (1966-1976), where the Chinese Communist Party intensified its attacks on Confucianism and Western influence pursing ideological purity (Bailey, 2001; Vohra, 2000). During the Cultural Revolution the discrediting of traditional education intensified, and ideological moderation was actively suppressed so as to create a classless society that valued equality, conformity, and self-sacrifice for collective interests (Ladany, 1988). The early Cultural Revolution was a period of extreme poverty resulting from the civil disorder created by radical political and social experiments (Yao, 2000). Reinstatement of moderate Deng Xiaoping as Vice Premier in 1972 restored a measure of societal and economic order (Bailey, 2001), and Mao Zedong's death in 1976 signaled the end of China's Cultural Revolution (Egri & Ralston, 2004).

The fifth generation is the Social Reform Era (1978 to present). The cultural values of this generation demonstrate substantial changes. During this era individual achievement, materialism, economic efficiency, and entrepreneurship have been encouraged (Tian, 1998). Due to an "Open Door" policy, Chinese business and education are having more influence from Western capitalistic ideologies (Vohra, 2000). China's emerging "network capitalism" represents a unique merger of Western market capitalism and collectivist values (Boisot & Child, 1996), with rapid industrialization and modernization resulting in unprecedented economic growth and prosperity (Tian, 1998; Yao, 2000). Although social reforms have brought Confucius back into official favor, Chinese youth who have grown up during the Social Reform Era have been described as: individualistic, materialistic, hedonistic, and entrepreneurial (Rosen, 1990).

Chinese political leaders have strengthened ties with the rest of the world, especially with the West, by participating in numerous political endeavors and in world issues. These relationships have opened a vast range of opportunities for the nation to establish and parley into economic leadership (Guthrie, 2006). The Eighth National Congress of the Communist Party of China initiated the economic reform in September 1956, launching the economic-management-system reform that allowed the country to move from a centrally planned economy to a market economy (Wu, 2005).

From the late 1970s, China has been known as a constantly changing country (Perkowski, 2008). By 1978 this market-oriented reform demanded the creation of private enterprises, which became the foundation of Chinese economy; "This is the most successful process in Chinese economic reform" (Perkowski, 2008, p. 54).

## Chinese Cultural Values

In brief, the cultural value that remains as the major influence in Chinese thinking and that makes for a practical and philosophical life style, as explained by Sheh (2002), is neo-Confucianism, a combination of Confucian humanism, Taoist naturalism, and Buddhist spirituality. Cultural values stress the importance of: harmony; persistence; interpersonal relationships; a serious awareness of one's present and potential enemies; recognizing trends and working with, rather than against, them; and long-term planning. Leaders are expected to model competence and especially outstanding moral character to keep followers' respect and loyalty.

A stable society focuses on the family in which each member sacrifices personal interests for those of the larger family unit and seeks to glorify the family name by working diligently while remaining frugal. The observance of etiquette influences interpersonal relationships. Using proper etiquette, hostility toward elders is suppressed, harmony is sought, aggression is disdained, conflict is eluded, and "face" must be gained and preserved. The Chinese people strive for excellence and public appreciation to develop and maintain a good name for themselves and their family. The Chinese person is aware that a highly-judgmental community is evaluating the leader's performance. The convictions or basic assumptions include the assurance that one's destiny is predetermined; thus, everything is related to everything else, and time works in a circular fashion. Good and bad times are expected by Chinese entrepreneurs, hoping to pass on their business to descendents for generations to come. Consequently, Chinese leadership style is characterized by a paternalistic style of leadership, strong emphasis on groups and collective behavior, strong family managerial roles and ownership, centralized decision-making, low structuring of activities such as unclear job descriptions, lines of authority, and communication. (Sheh, 2002).

Chinese leadership emphasizes the concept of authoritarian leadership, such that the follower prefers an authoritarian, yet benevolent and respected leader who is considerate of the followers, and is able to take skilled and decisive actions (Bond & Hwang, 1986; Redding & Wong, 1986). Although leaders of the state and corporations are no longer collectively viewed as "God-appointed," leaders have remained greatly separated from the governed. In this system of leadership, the governed have a "supernatural personal" relationship with their leaders (Farh & Cheng, 2000). Businesses are maintained in a family setting, where the leader seeks to gain wealth and status as sources of power, but also to care for family members, even if they do not fully deserve their care. The Chinese leader manages carefully limited resources and develops a web of relationships (*guan xi*) that expand the leader's authority, influence and capacity (Sheh, 2002).

## China Today

A brief exploration of China today reveals Chinese business leaders evolving and impacting their country and the world. China has a very rich culture and heritage. The nation has withstood wars, foreign occupations, famines, and economic crises, but manages to stand strong. A member of the world's recognized superpowers, the nation is one of the few remaining communist states in the world, but its recognition of efforts to participate in global enterprise and trade has significantly altered the country's economic condition. Its vast land area and resources, rich population, and continuous efforts in research and development have launched the republic into one of the most powerful economic leaders in the world today (Central Intelligence Agency, 2010). The Chinese people have encouraged foreigners into their borders for education, and even to supply new capital for investments. But the principles of the nation, leadership, and citizenship have managed to remain intact even until today.

These principles strengthen critical aspects of Chinese leadership, not just in the state, but also in the leadership of businesses and firms (Ralston, Holt, Terpstra, & Cheng, 2007).

How China rose from crisis to take its place as one of the world's most powerful economic leaders has largely been attributed to the model of management and leadership that has been observed in Chinese company and state leadership (Naughton, 2007).

*Market Economy*

China is observed to be successfully moving into a market-based economy wherein it is able to accept the usual uncertainty and risks that business leaders encounter to meet the demands of the consumer. According to Malik (1997), "each party is willing to accept the responsibility of failure that comes with uncertainty in the areas of production, consumption, policy making and implementation" (p. 155). Strengthening the market through liberalization has emphasized private firms and companies, thereby strengthening their leaders as well. Managers of companies, in a sense, were granted more power and control over their enterprises because of the independence that the state grants to them (Chow, 2007). Economic freedom has placed significant pressure on leaders to deliver and answer the needs of the economy, and this has encouraged leaders to assume responsibility to study the workings of business enterprises. In effect, the Chinese brand of leadership became empowered by education and technical proficiency (Byham, 2009). Diversification of management styles and leader attitudes is also an effect brought about by changes in politics and economics. Political and economic openness to the West spurred the influx of cross-cultural references in leadership strategies and styles such that some Chinese leaders follow a hybrid of traditional Chinese leadership and Western-management style (Yasheng, 1990).

Park and Vanhonacker (2007) explained that since the opening of the Chinese economy to foreign investment, and later in 2001 when they joined the World Trade Organization, the Chinese government and consumers have changed their perceptions of Multinational Corporations (MNCs). China's development has been significantly impacted by the contributions of MNCs. In 2004 they produced 57 percent of all exports from China, 28 percent of industrial output from China, and 19 percent tax revenue (Park & Vanhonacker, 2007, p. 8). Furthermore, recently the government reported that approximately 85 percent of intellectual-property rights used in China are owned by MNCs (Park & Vanhonacker, 2007).

One of the MNCs that started a history with China even before their economic reform is the Siemens ® Company. Siemens® was founded in 1847, when W. von Siemens and J. G. Halske established a Telegraph Construction Company in Berlin, Germany. Today the Siemens® Group has more than 400,000 employees and business activities in 190 countries, with reported consolidated revenue of €76.651 billion in fiscal year 2009 (Siemens, 2010a). Their history with China dates back to 1872 when Siemens® delivered China's first pointer telegraph. Today in Siemens Ltd., China, there are more than 30,000 employees and, for fiscal year 2009, sales to customers in China amounted to €5.2 billion and new orders totaled €5.5 billion (Siemens, 2010a, para. 3). At the beginning of 2010 Siemens® was recognized as one of the top ten most influential multinational companies in China by the Chinese Central Television (CCTV), the leading national television organization of China (Siemens, 2010b). Consequently, for an integrated company that is in daily contact with customers around the world, diversity is a success factor. Siemens (2010a) launched the Siemens Diversity Initiative to ensure management positions are filled with the best possible people, representing a global talent pool and reflecting the diversity of the company's customers and younger employees. R. Hausmann[1] (personal communication, Beijing, March 24, 2010), President of Siemens Ltd. China, further stressed that:

> The economic impact in China comes from MNCs and international companies that import and export from and to China more of 50% of the available product. As a result, China overflows with new products, giving to the Chinese population many options and more contact with a worldwide market. In addition, China's economy is influenced primarily by the desire of its residents to acquire *a status*, which is reflected in the way they think as buyers: expensive is good. A good example of this consumer behavior is observed in the car market, as expensive cars have become more popular in the Chinese market during the last five years.

## Leadership Development

R. Hausmann explained that MNCs have existed for a number of years in China and the evolution of Chinese business leaders has been influenced greatly by them. Hausmann stated, "In effect, at the present time we can observe an economic society moving into a European management style, as well as a new generation of

---

[1] R. Hausmann was honored with the Yellow Crane Friendship Award in Wuhan, China, which is the highest acclamation from Wuhan Municipal Government to expatriates. Hausmann also received the Great Wall Friendship Award of Beijing and the Golden Magnolia Award of Shanghai for contributions to the development of the country. R. Hausmann resided as Advisor of Foreign Trade and Economic Cooperation to Shenyang and held several positions including Chairman of the Executive Committee of Foreign Invested Companies in China, Chairman of the Board of German Chamber of Commerce in China, and is currently a member of the International Consultant of Wuhan Municipal Government.

students who focus mainly on the business leader's style of a Western Society" (personal communication, March 24, 2010). Moreover, Kinge, McGregor, Pilling, Dickie, and Authers (2010) explained that China will continue to be influenced by Western and European styles of leadership, integrating it into their own style. Military spending will continue to slow, because China does not anticipate becoming a superlative military power. China will continue looking for a peaceful market-economy evolution.

R. A. Altamirano, Financial Advisor for the Consulate General of Ecuador in Shanghai (personal communication, March 28, 2010) clarified:

> China's economy has changed from an external economy to an internal economy and domestic consumption is growing really fast. Progress in many areas of the economy is quite fast, but there are areas that require a clear improvement, like healthcare system, which at this time is a challenge. Medical service needs development. The government has restricted foreign investment and government regulations do not allow doctors to be part of private hospitals financed by foreign investment. There are still practices that need improvement and areas for smokers that even smoke in hospitals and clinics. Also, another important aspect of China's changes is in education. In China education has great importance and is becoming a growth industry. A clear example of this change is education in foreign languages. Chinese families spend much effort, time, and money for their children to learn new languages; it is not uncommon to see families spending weekends, Saturdays and Sundays, to bring their children to private schools or teachers to learn a new language.

China is developing the next generation of Chinese business leaders and returning them to school; because of globalization and the demands of the new economy, companies expect more educated and skilled executives (Byham, 2009; Chao, 2007). The future of Chinese companies relies on the ability of their leaders to succeed (Saenz, 2006). As further explained by Chao (2007), China's leading firms are enrolling in the MBA or e-MBA programs in China. In September 2002, the Ministry of Education allowed 30 of the top business schools to launch e-MBA programs under the supervision of the Ministry of Education and the Peking, Shanghai Jiao Tong and Fudan Universities.

The government allows the country's business schools to partner with international schools, resulting in a massive influx of foreign business schools into China. These international schools are addressing different needs, not only to educate Chinese business leaders to operate their businesses as businesses rather than as organizations with a goal, but also to address the need of Chinese business leaders to better understand executives and businessmen from the rest of the world as Chinese companies go overseas (Chao, 2007). They also support leaders attending to the recent emerging role of global information technology and business-service outsourcing, which are fully supported by the government (Wright, 2009).

## Population

In this fashion, Chinese population trends are changing at the same speed of its economy. The rural population will drop in the next three decades from the current 900 million to 400 million as young emigrant workers are reluctant to go back to the countryside (Jin, 2010, p. 3). Young emigrants would rather stay in the cities, even if the salaries are so low that they cannot enjoy any services offered by the cities. In contrast, the average expenditure on a wedding was ¥ 30,000 to 40,000 ($4,440–$5,900) in 2009, compared with ¥ 20,000 in 2005; yet professional wedding services have increased, especially in hotels (Jin, 2010, p. 3). The real-estate market is burgeoning in China. In large, popular cities an apartment with three or four rooms (265 sqm; 2,852 ft²) rents monthly for ¥ 20,000 ($2,943); some amenities include a garden or in-floor heat, and a Western name, such as Rancho Santa Fe (Real State, 2010, p. B7).

The Chinese one-child policy introduced in 1978, as the government restricted the number of children per family to one, according to the Chinese authorities, has been considered a great success in helping to implement China's current economic growth, reducing many problems that result from overpopulation. Some problems that have been overcome include social services—education, health, and law enforcement—unemployment rates, increased savings and investments by the population, and producing income from wealthy families, who paid fines to have another child. The negative impact on the Chinese society includes first, women under the pressure to produce a single male child and one child responsible for two parents and two grandparents, putting too much economic pressure on one person. Then, these only children are overindulged, called "little emperors," sometimes leading to poor social communication skills vital for relating to others and being productive in an adult environment. A result is the social instability as the female population diminishes, due to the social preference for sons, based on Confucianism and rural and urban incentives. It is estimated that by 2020 there will be 30 million more men than women (Hu, 2002).

## Chinese Economy and Leadership in USA

China is a hybrid between market and centrally planned economy with very high influence from the state. Through its policies, the government continued to influence investment challenges which have over time evolved from restrictions to encouragement and thus the increase of Chinese business leaders in global markets like the United States (Yi & Ye, 2003). The first stage of restricted outward investment to the United States was marked in approximately 1979

(Jones, 2010). Between the years 1984 and 1992, non-state firms were allowed to discriminatively invest in overseas markets, a move that saw the onset of a few Chinese business leaders into the United States. In the years 1993-1998, outward investments were highly tightened, hence increasing business investments to the United States. The Chinese government explained the reason to this move being the need to make sure that the overseas investments were productive in terms of benefiting China in terms of income (Zhao, 2008).

The year 1999 saw the aggressive onset of the go global campaign encouraging Chinese firms to be beneficial in driving China's export drive. The government supported private firms by eliminating unnecessary control in the reserves at the foreign exchange. Administrative procedures were also simplified to emphasize this support. Until today the go global campaign is still being advanced. It has been proven that in China the government and its policies are important guides as well as supporters of the Chinese to venture in developed markets especially for emerging and inexperienced businessmen (Chen, 2004). These companies over time have grown from household industries and companies to multi-corporations that bring to China billions of dollars as pretax profits every year. As markets started getting saturated at the home, various large corporations started branching out to gain first mover advantage in unexplored markets or markets with little competition (Jones, 2010). Yi and Ye (2003) mention another reason for the growth of these businesses as the depletion of raw materials due to China's trade and tremendous growth exhibited. They discuss that China started making trade ties with resource rich nations especially in the United States and Europe in order to secure supplies. This led the Chinese companies to invest in developed markets; for example, Haier opening up a plant in the United States in 1999. In order to maintain the trademark of the name or company operations, the companies send experienced managers from their old branches in China so that they can overlook the running of the companies with the Chinese style and trademark. Zhao (2008) considers this to ensure Chinese companies are managed in a unique way from the other dominant companies in the United States and other markets. Though these leaders use a different management style to that of the United States businesses, they sometimes learn the operations and other factors that are different from theirs so as to blend their organization culture with the employees' needs (Yi & Ye, 2003).

China has invested abroad heavily in established markets like the United States (Brousseau, Ho, & Tseng, 2005). Child and Rodrigues (2005) examined the patterns and internalization motives by market seeking demand firms. They found out that Chinese firms are just seeking brand and technological assets in order to establish a competitive place in international markets. Child and Rodrigues (2005) further present that Chinese business leaders have continued collaboration with leaders from other nations as they understand how other markets operate. So far Chinese managers of Chinese firms in the United States are doing very well in expanding their products (Ibid).

China and the United States business managers have significantly different leadership styles (Hoivik, 2007). Cross-cultural research findings illustrate that when American business managers are compared with Chinese managers, Chinese managers tend to avoid ambiguity at whatever cost, as well as they have long-term goals (Hofstede, 2007). The American managers on the other hand have short-term goals, are specific, masculine, and have a positive attitude towards uncertainty. American managers also confront problems head-on and often have a resistance towards investing in procedural assistance unless it can straightforwardly affect the target (Ibid). Brousseau et al. (2005) consider Chinese managers resistant to handle uncertainty and in most cases, they depend on third party help.

Brousseau et al. (2005) argued that Chinese leaders highly stress on interpersonal relations since they consider them to be important influencers of employees. Most of these managers hence use gifts to attain the influence. Zhang and Alon (2009) on the opposite side explain that American businesses consider giving gifts as bad blood or a form of corruption which can easily attract legal action. The main uniqueness of Chinese businesses, Confucianism, has been reported to lose ground in some managers due to foreign influence, particularly from United States business managers (Ibid). Those managers still working in China did not show such shift (Zhang & Alon, 2009). This means that some of the business leaders are starting to shift in favor of the influence they get from the market they are exposed to.

Around the world, decision-making has been identified as the key element that differentiates managers as well as businesses (Hoivik, 2007). The decision-making, on the other hand, is significantly affected by the social and the business environment. The American decision-making style shows a high need for achievement, while that of the Chinese Business leaders found their decisions on practicing and maintaining power (Hirahara, 2003). What this means is that the United States business leaders make decisions that address the challenges or establishment of opportunities for appreciation. American business leaders are more likely to come up with solutions for possible problems, hence inducing a decision-making process that is formalized and structured. Hoivik (2007) further argues that the Chinese's exercise of maintaining power in decision-making makes them have a high degree of control. This method may be well seen, but when the company merges with the American business leaders, a conflict is initiated, something that may not favor business performance. It should be noted that continuous variation in decision-making styles inhibits exchange of information among managers since apart from their unwillingness to learn from each other; they have different managerial beliefs and practices (Hoivik, 2007).

Uncertainty avoidance (the process of the society/business managers identifying ways to avoid uncertainties) is another thing that differentiates the strategy of Chinese firms from United States firms (Brousseau et al., 2005). According to Hoivik (2007), Chinese business leaders tend to have very high uncertain avoidance when matched to their American counterparts. The high uncertainty avoidance is characteristic of numerous planning and comprehensive agreements. Low uncertain avoidance environments have more flexibility and innovation, which allows employees to develop their own problem-solving skills (Hoivik, 2007).

During the 90s, Chinese citizens started rising in the business world (Jones, 2010). In America, Chinese small businesses, like restaurants, grew rapidly to cater to the specific needs of the Chinese-Americans living in some states. Chen (2004) reckons that the growth of Chinese businesses in the United States was a result of the needs Chinese saw in the United States market. Jones (2010) observes that the Chinese saw the United States market being provided with highly priced goods. Based on the Chinese's good understanding of the cultural, environmental and economic factors of the United States population, it was expected that a better and highly competitive business sector would be born out of the imported knowledge and experience of businesses to the United States (Chen, 2004).

There are several restraints that are slowing down the success of Chinese businesses in America or other established global markets. Zhao (2008) argues that inexperienced managers as well as staff in the operations department of a company in new, foreign-established markets impede the journey to successful businesses. Business leaders cannot also scale the talent that will be successful in the American Market. Zhao (2008) notes that to curb these problems the Chinese business leaders are trying out some techniques which are improving their success rate in the American market. Zhao (2008) adds that Chinese companies are sending their best and most promising managers to multinational managed business schools for intensive training programs in order to have well trained staff who are loyal to the company and can effectively manage offices in America and elsewhere. Zhang and Alon (2009) credit the effective management Chinese managers are likely to have on the capability of these multinational business schools to train their students on different business environments.

To establish their global reach, Chinese business leaders have also taken to buying into and/or acquiring established local and international companies. For example, Lenovo bought IBM's unit of personal computers at a cost of $1.35 billion (Gallo, 2011). This is because buying into an established brand ensures acceptance and an already established market such that in case ownership changes, the brand which is more important remains. However, in some situations the Chinese have been unsuccessful in buying into existing businesses. An instance of this is the $18.5 billion bid for the United States oil company, UNOCAL that was unsuccessful (Jones, 2010).

Jones (2010) writes that Chinese business leaders have had a very big advantage in targeting and enticing new and old markets due to the fact that they have been dealing with emerging market consumers. Gallo (2011) observes that Chinese business leaders are deemed to gain success from keeping their cost of production low, hence producing low priced goods that are of the desired quality. This strategy has significantly boosted the Chinese business growth in the United States (Hofstede, 2007). However, as Chinese companies globalize, the Chinese business leaders are also facing challenges besides their successes in terms of communication and culture across the United States (Zhang & Alon, 2009). Many of the big Chinese company leaders are not fluent in English, and therefore when set to head overseas companies they have to work with a translator before getting used to the language (Gallo, 2011). Yi and Ye (2003), however, advise that to increase the speed of global acculturation, Chinese leaders should plan ahead, for example, by introducing intensive training and extensive programs for senior staff to help bridge communication and cultural barriers.

Research shows that Chinese businesses are significant in the United States. There have been several meetings between the Chinese business leaders and government officials and those from the West, which show that China is positively influencing the business market in

America (Chen, 2004). In July 2009, the first strategic and economic dialogue was held in Washington DC. This meeting was attended by the United States cabinet officials and 15 Chinese ministers; both United States and Chinese business leaders and vice minister discussed issues of the global economic crisis. Timothy Geither, treasury secretary, stated that the government highly appreciated the corporation between the two entities and hoped that the relationship would grow not only for the financial health of both nations but also that of the global economy (Gallo, 2011).

In order to bring about sustainability of the global economy, Zhao (2008) opines that several policies were to be undertaken. This led to the United States and China agreeing to establish a framework of cooperation based on four major issues. The issues were: promotion of open market, oriented and resilient financial systems, strengthening of investment, and trade between the two entities. Strengthening of financial architecture internationally and advancement of macroeconomic and structural policies are some of the things that enhance business growth between these two nations. This shows that the United States is interested in increasing the level of China's involvement in financial institutions at an international level (Zhao, 2008).

According to Hirahara (2003), the Chinese businessmen started making ripples in the United States economy even before China as a country started merging with other developed economies. One of the business leaders and entrepreneurs doing well in the current American market is Ren Zhengfei, founder and C.E.O of HUAWEI technologies. He is a well-respected Chinese businessman. Starting small in China among telecommunication giants like Alcatel in 1988, the business has risen to one of the most respected telecommunication empires, employing a staff of over 620,000 all over the world, and the leading equipment vendor in the global market, servicing 31 of the top 50 telecom operators. With foreign investments totaling over US$178 billion, Ren was honored in the *Times* among the "Builders and Titans" (Hirahara, 2003; Zhang & Alon, 2009).

Other significant business leaders are: Shi Zhengrong, the founder and president of the worldwide leading solar energy company, Suntech Power Holdings Co., Ltd, currently listed in the New York stock exchange; Shi Stan, the founder of one of the oldest and well-respected top computer companies, Acer; Rong Zhijiang and his father, who are the major shareholders of the CITIC group, which after investing in the United States in 1982 cooperated with IBM engineers establishing an Automation Design Company, the first company to specialize in computer aided software (Zhang & Alon, 2009).

A number of acculturation scales instruments have been developed to assess specific ethnic groups, such as Asian Americans— the Suinn-Lew Asian Self-Identity Acculturation Scale SL-ASIA (Suinn et al., 1992); and Chinese Americans—the General Ethnic Questionnaire-Chinese version (Tsai, 2000). The SL-ASIA scale originally consisted of 21 multiple-choice questions that covered: language, identity, friendship choice, behaviors, generation/ geographic history, and attitudes. In the most recent version, Questions 21 to 26 were added to further classify participants in ways that use current theorizing multi-dimensional and orthogonal, and not linear or uni-dimensional (Suinn et al., 1992). The SL-ASIA has been applied to Asian groups such as Vietnamese Americans (Duan & Vu, 2000), Chinese Americans (Tata & Leong, 1994), and Japanese Americans (Atkinson & Matsushita, 1991) based on samples composed of college students. Further, the use of one scale for all Asian groups may not reflect the cultural qualities of a specific group (Suinn et al., 1987) such as the Chinese. According to the authors, it appears that a different scale for each specific Asian group is more appropriate in the same way as is necessary to design separate instruments for Hispanics groups such as Mexicans and Cubans. Moreover, Duan and Vu (2000) stated that the scale fails to identify situational behaviors, and this limitation is particularly significant since situational behavior is a characteristic of Chinese culture.

Chinese immigrants experience multiple difficulties when they arrive and try to adjust to life in the United States, however, many of them attain social and financial success not only within their ethnic community but in the American social environment as well (Mizokawa & Ryckman, 1990; Sue & Okazaki, 1990). Chinese immigrants carry cultural values that emphasize high resilience, such as: *collectivism,* the inclination to prioritize group needs over individual needs (Hofstede, 1980); *relational orientation,* where the self is defined through continuous interdependence with others (Yee, Debaryshe, Yuen, Kim, & McCubbin, 1998); and *family obligation,* where the younger generation is expected to demonstrate respect, obedience and continual care of the children and elders' wellbeing (Chao & Tseng, 2002; Xu, Xie, Liu, Xia, & Liu, 2007). These values, endorsed by older Chinese generations, are the significant factor of resilience in Chinese immigrants (Yeh, Kim, Pituc, & Atkins, 2008). New Chinese immigrants face the pressure to acculturate into the Western culture in order to survive; they encounter major changes in: communication, social support network, role within their family, job, and education (Zhou, 1997). Even first generation immigrants can be exposed to American European values from interaction with college peers and the general academia setting (Biesta, 2007). Research regarding Chinese immigrants' resiliency has suggested that first generation immigrants demonstrate highly resilient behaviors in a foreign country because of the traditional "hard work and effort equals success" value that is essential and central in Chinese cultures (Plucker, 1994; Siu & Shek, 2005).

*New Generation of Chinese Leaders*

In ancient China leaders were viewed as the appointees of the gods, and were set to rule under the *Mandate of Heaven.* Thus their legitimacy and authority over the people was not questioned. As leaders under that mandate, they exercised their power working for the good of the people and forwarding the benevolence of the gods in heaven (Chen, 2002; Schell, 1994). Thus, Chinese philosophical principles have placed leaders above the common people, minimizing the rights of the individual (Pye, 1991). At that time, citizens of the nation were to put their full trust in their leaders and do everything they could to follow whatever was ordered and asked of them by the state, because it was their assigned tasks and specializations that fulfilled their role in the whole-society mandate. Men of the nation were given the responsibility to produce food for the nation, govern units of society, and defend the empire if another party dared destabilize the order of society; whereas women were to bear and care for the children, care for their husbands, and maintain the household. The meritocracy system, where responsibilities are assigned to individuals based on demonstrated abilities and intelligence, was not fully appreciated in Chinese society because the culture dictated that certain dynasties of elites continued to be leaders. Because of this lack of credit to skilled individuals, stagnancy described those who did not belong to a certain class; therefore, it was difficult for someone to climb to higher leadership by mere merit alone.

Most leaders in the Chinese society came from the same family or group of elites (Bachman, 1992). The citizens and the governed still hold that the leaders will always work to drive the group toward an end that is benevolent, and this thought serves as a restriction against placing themselves as important, like their higher leaders (Zhao, 2009). On the other hand, an alienated culture, which does not give credit to individuals in recognition of their merits, has negative repercussions. According to Hwang (1997), ambitious members of society who want to climb through the ranks take on a strategy that involves strengthening the ties they have with a leader through any means possible; thus, working for a leader's favor just to gain authority and recognition is common in Chinese society.

However, Krug and Pólos (2000) stated that the very *Chineseness* of Chinese entrepreneurship has resulted in successful economic reforms and sustaining economic efficacy despite working through an economic construct that may be contradictory to that of the Western economy. Conversely, it was posited that in its most extreme manifestation, it is the very "Chineseness" of the culture that allows

Chinese people to be entrepreneurial. There is a dichotomy in Chinese economic perspectives, and some believe that the traditional Chinese business culture is outdated and counterproductive; others assert that it is the very basis of China's economic success (Alon & Shenkar, 2003). Moreover, R. Hausmann (personal communication, March 24, 2010), current president and Chief Executive Officer (CEO) of Siemens Ltd. China, based on day-to-day interaction with Chinese government and Chinese business leaders, elucidated that Chinese business leaders have their own leadership style with special characteristics that identify their leadership style:

> Their leadership style works together with their cultural background, with their way of thinking as individuals, but also as a group. We can see that Confucianism continues to be a major influence and they develop an intense *guanxi* as a way to relate to others.

R. Hausmann further clarified,

> Chinese business leaders manage under hierarchy structures and a strong person is usually who leads at the international arena. At the present time Chinese business leaders have a strong relationship with the Chinese Communist Party, as they are political people. Real Chinese business leaders are members of their political party. The Party has an incredible way to motivate and develop members to become leaders; their practices, management, and methods support the development of leaders, for example a 360 degree feedback.

M. Oechsner, General Manager of Siemens Gas Turbine Parts Ltd. In Shanghai (personal communication, March, 2010) exposed that:

> Chinese workforce is learning to develop a leadership style. They do not display a leadership style as a result of Western leadership training and influence as they do as

a member of the political party. Chinese workforce in general embraces more followers than leaders.

G. Matuschek, Commercial Project Manager of Siemens Power Equipment Packages Co., Ltd. in Shanghai (personal communication, March, 2010) confirmed that "Chinese business leaders have their own leadership style as they are a different population, with their own concept of freedom and performance; they truly believe if other person can do it, I can do it too." Matuschek further explained that Chinese leaders "know where they want to be in five, ten or twenty years, and that they will be there since their business strategies are not only short or middle term, their strategies are a long term." Matuschek's impression of Chinese business people is that "they are successful people that are probably more capitalist than the rest of the world." Furthermore, F. Karpinski, Director Procurement Products China of Siemens Power Equipment Package Co., Ltd. (personal communication, March, 2010) clarified that in order to do business with Chinese business people it is necessary to build a relationship based on trust. Karpinski assured that:

> There [are] not many people with experience; they have education but not experience. It is a new generation of business people. Their leadership style is different: they are followers who are learning to adapt. I had applied the same basic management techniques that I had applied before in Germany as motivation, support, feedback, and trust, and I have results; it takes more time but is working.

Fernandez and Underwood (2006) asserted that any business executive who regularly travels to China will acknowledge that the nation is revolutionizing its path in a transformation that embraces market capitalism rather than a planned economy. This transformative process is the transition from a traditionally Chinese construct to one that is more compatible with the Western world.

Under this transformative process, Chinese enterprises would share similar characteristics with their non-Chinese counterparts over time, although the former may still be able to uphold certain particularities or idiosyncrasies. (Wong, 2008, p. 152)

J. Eichhorst, Chief Financial Officer of Siemens Ltd. China Shanghai branch for Power Generation Group and Chief Financial Officer of Shanghai Electric Power Generation Equipment Co. Ltd., remarked that:

Chinese business leaders are focus oriented and they are eager to accomplish their goals. Management implementation has a top down approach under a seniority principle. We need to remember that in every part of the world the Chinese people are Chinese and in China any project developed with Chinese people always will have that special Chinese feature (Personal communication, Shanghai, March, 2010).

An empirical study (Wah, 2002), honored by the Maastricht School of Management, the Netherlands, suggested that Chinese transformational leaders blend their contemporary leadership practices with their rich cultural values. This empirical study uncovered eight key behavioral attributes of the transformational Chinese leader. These attributes are comparable to those in the Western literature: visionary leadership, willingness to take risks, ability to communicate, possess good execution power, be a life-long learner, and possess a high sense of achievement (Wah, 2002). Furthermore, Lowe (2003) suggested that it is possible to integrate Western theories of management with some of the existing Chinese values to present a viable leadership theory.

Heberer and Gluckman (2003) considered that the success of transformative leadership in China exhibited the positive impact of privatization by: (a) creating and improving political responsibility and social participation, (b) reducing governmental intervention, (c) contributing to the privatization of social life because fundamental aspects like education, housing, and training are decided by families and individuals rather than the state, (d) making society more independent, (e) strengthening the business elite against the political elite, (f) stressing the perspective of privatization safeguarding rights, freedom of occupation, contracts and associations, and (g) further developing the legal system. Many of these virtues reflect the same belief in freedom and independence that can be found in capitalistic tenets and methodologies.

Such a heavy transition with such serious implications requires business leaders to be highly influential and instrumental in China's economic development (Yeung, 2008). As validation to this point, and as previously referenced in Chapter One, Cheng (2005) expanded the research for the transformation of Chinese leaders by indicating the rapid rise of Chinese entrepreneurs that has been matched by the remarkable development of China's economy. Cheng's study analyzed the biographical information of current CEOs of the top 100 companies in China, which was derived from the National Association of Chinese Enterprises, an organization that ranks the largest business firms in China primarily based on their total revenues in 2004. The corporations included in this list represent a wide range of industries and vary in type of ownership, although a majority of them are state-owned and/or shareholding enterprises. Cheng's study indicated that a group of young, well-educated, urban elites—China's "yuppie corps"—has recently emerged and come to prominence.

A few distinguished members of this new elite group have already become CEOs of four leading companies in China. All four of these Chinese firms are ranked by Fortune magazine as top companies in the Global 500. The characteristics and worldviews of the executives of China's leading corporations not only will influence the trajectory of economic development in the country, but also will have ramifications far beyond China's border. Furthermore, these elites from the China's top business firms are also mentoring leaders in the next generation of Chinese political leadership. The CEOs of China's leading corporations usually have the official government rank of vice minister or vice provincial governor or higher. At the 16th National Congress of the CCP, held in 2002, for the first time in history entrepreneurs of large enterprises and banks attended as distinct groups. The relatively young age of China's top business leaders and the growing importance of their enterprises indicate that this new elite group is likely to play a more pivotal political leadership role in the near future. The top 100 firms listed in Cheng's (2005) study are considered titans in the Chinese economy as well as remarkably prominent on the world stage.

For Chinese companies to compete successfully in the globalized economy of the twenty-first century, further changes must be made (Sheh, 2002). Chinese organizations are often harmed by overbearing, authoritarian leadership; micromanagement; unclear roles and rules; favoritism; fierce competition among subordinates; and poor communication, especially from the bottom to the top. Furthermore, Chinese citizens reflect their larger social, cultural, and political reality; they are not trained to be independent thinkers, nor direct and vocal advocates for their individual viewpoints, especially when facing figures of authority (Liu, 2008). Educated Chinese who return to China to work in Chinese companies usually are treated with hostility, as locals perceive them to be favored by managers; thus, companies are adjusting the process of repatriation with a reintegration program to avoid resentment from coworkers (Tess Lyons, 2005). Moreover, middle managers do not make decisions or have power, inhibiting the process of managers becoming leaders (Tess Lyons, 2005). Therefore, the ongoing makeover of its economy signifies that Chinese business leaders must wield or acquire a skill-set that merges new methods with the old (Fan, 1995). There is a need to improve business leadership in China, as elucidated by Gallo (2008). Chinese business leaders are relatively new in business, yet they are being asked to manage their people in a market economy when the focus of planned economic leaders is towards the Party and government instead of towards the employees.

Chinese business leader research by the Boston Consulting Group at the Wharton School (Strategic Management, 2005) implied that local Chinese business leaders are changing their behavior and assuming greater roles in the management ranks. Moreover, a study from HayGroup (2007) revealed that Chinese business leaders possess many competences and skills that will continue taking their businesses and economy forward. These skills have supported them to success so far, yet Chinese business leaders continue to build a sense of innovation to respond inventively to demand. Also, they need to develop the skills to recognize, develop, and nurture talent, evolving their leadership style.

In brief, Kuhn (2010) advised that the best way to know China and their leaders is to understand what motivates them and what guides their policies. Understanding how China's leaders think gives us a better understanding of their culture. The last three decades of reform and opening to the Western economy has given Chinese leaders great opportunities, yet much uncertainty. Kuhn spoke with Chinese leaders from different Internet/state-owned companies, from healthcare to religion, and concluded that a new China model is emerging rather than the so-called China-threat. Furthermore, Kuhn confronted leaders on China's problems, such us "economic imbalances, environmental pollution, unsustainable development, human rights, democracy, rule of law, media censorship, corruption, crime, unemployment, migrant worker minorities, ethnic conflicts, religious tension, social instability, protests and demonstrations, ideological shake-up, shifting moral and family values, death penalty, organs from executed prisoners, global confrontations, resource competition, military expansion, and the impact of the worldwide financial crisis," (p. XV) to acknowledge the long road China must still travel to realize President Hu Jintao's vision of a Harmonious Society. "There is a deep conviction that China must never repeat its errors of the past and a fervent expectation that the country's long future is bright and ascendant" (Kuhn, 2010, p. XV).

Finally, despite China's strict political system, Shen (2010) pointed out that the world has been impressed by its capabilities. The last two worldwide events have shown China's organizational capacity to the world. The Beijing Olympics 2008 and the Shanghai EXPO 2010 "Better City, Better Life" are the envy of other countries. Expo visitors totaled more than 67 million during the six-month event. More than 190 countries and 50 international organizations were registered to participate (Expo 2010 Shanghai China, 2008). Through these events the Chinese government exhibited to Chinese people its openness to the outside world, and showed the world its modernization, symbolizing China's integration with the world.

## *Discussion, Interpretation and Recommendations*

In investigating the relationship between acculturation and leadership style/practices of Chinese business leaders living and working in the United States, the researcher examined leadership in its different views and categories, acculturation and acculturation of Chinese business leaders in the United States. Further, a deep analysis of the two-phase sequential mixed method design was used along with quantitative and qualitative methods to collect and analyze numerical data and text. The quantitative data was collected from two reliable and valid survey instruments: the Suinn-Lew Asian Self Identity Acculturation scale (SL-ASIA) scale, and the Multifactor Leadership Questionnaire (MLQ-5X), along with the demographics.

The Suinn-Lew Asian Self Identity Acculturation scale (SL-ASIA) is an instrument that measures acculturation among Asian Americans. There are four separate acculturation scores in this instrument.

## Discussion and Interpretation

The discussion and interpretation for this study reflected the self-perception of the Chinese business leaders who agreed to participate in this study. The researcher formulated conclusions using the quantitative, qualitative, and triangulation data analysis, as well as the literature review.

## Research Question 1

*What are the correlations between acculturation score determined by the Suinn-Lew Asian Self Identity Acculturation scale (SL-ASIA) and the leadership style/practices as defined by the Multifactor Leadership Questionnaire (MLQ-5X)?*

The findings of this study suggested that acculturation scores have a significant correlation with leadership style/practices. Further, that the number of correlations between acculturation and leadership styles is larger with the transformational leadership style. Additionally, the findings exposed a significant correlation between self-identity and outcomes of leadership.

Furthermore, the leadership attributes and behaviors revealed by participants in Phase One, and supported with the interviews in Phase Two, exhibit important scores in transformational and transactional leadership styles and behaviors.

In brief, participants displayed higher scores in transformational leadership attributes such us idealized influence (IIA) going beyond self-interest for the good of the group; inspirational motivation (IM) expressing enthusiasm and confidence in the goals to achieve; and intellectual stimulation (IS) re-examining and suggesting ways to address problems.

The following table identified the scores for participants that exhibit the highest values in transformational leadership styles and behaviors. For example, participant 6 exhibited the highest score (mean = 3.820), and Participant 10 the lowest score (mean =2.920). Further, the scores identified for cultural behaviors for the same participants revealed that Participant 9 exhibited the highest score (mean= 3.76), and Participant 1 the lowest score (mean=1.67). data supported with interviews as participants provide details that support this data.

*MLQ-5X and SL-ASIA Quantitative Scores by Participant*

| Participants | MLQ-5X | | | SL-ASIA | | | |
|---|---|---|---|---|---|---|---|
| | Transformational Leadership | Transactional | Passive/ Avoidant | Cultural Behaviors | Values | Behavioral Competences | Self-Identity |
| | Mean 3.02** | Mean 2.29** | Mean 0.84** | Mean 2.13*** | Mean 4.05*** | Mean 4.35*** | Mean 2.60*** |
| P1 | 3.03 | 2.30 | 0.00 | 1.67 | 4.50 | 5.00 | 1.00 |
| P2 | 3.08 | 2.80 | 0.00 | 2.14 | 4.00 | 4.50 | 1.00 |
| P3 | 3.58 | 3.00 | 0.90 | 2.29 | 4.00 | 4.50 | 5.00 |
| P4 | 3.16 | 3.40 | 1.30 | 2.05 | 4.00 | 4.00 | 1.00 |
| P5 | 3.28 | 2.25 | 1.30 | 3.48 | 4.00 | 5.00 | 3.00 |
| P6 | **3.82*** | 2.50 | 1.30 | 2.86 | 4.00 | 4.00 | 5.00 |
| P7 | 3.58 | 2.30 | 1.50 | 2.52 | 4.00 | 4.00 | 3.00 |
| P8 | 2.58 | 2.90 | 1.25 | 1.95 | 4.50 | 4.00 | 1.00 |
| P9 | 3.00 | 0.00 | 0.50 | **3.76*** | 3.50 | 4.00 | 5.00 |
| P10 | 2.92 | 2.50 | 0.30 | 2.33 | 4.00 | 4.50 | 1.00 |

* Highest mean by participants from MLQ-5X and SL-ASIA scores by participant.

** The mean utilized in this table for the MLQ-5X is calculated based on the means provided by the Descriptive Statistics for MLQ 5X 2004 Normative Sample – MLQ Table 10. (US), Column Self, by B. Avolio, B. Bass, F.O. Walumbwa, and W. Zhu, 2004, Third Edition Manual and Sampler Set, p. 69 (Appendix G). MLQ

Manual Copyright 1995, 2000, 2004 by Bernard Bass and Bruce Avolio. Published by Mind Garden, Inc.

*** Mean based on scores provided by participants in SL-ASIA.

*Research Question 2*

*What is the acculturation score determined by the Suinn-Lew Asian Self Identity Acculturation scale (SL-ASIA) for the business leaders that exhibit a transformational leadership style/practices as defined by the Multifactor Leadership Questionnaire (MLQ-5X)?*

The descriptive statistics for the Multifactor Leadership Questionnaire (MLQ-5X) showed that the highest scored scale of the participants in the sample was the transformational scale. The transformational scale mean was 3.20 (sd = 0.37), implying the majority of the responses ranged between *fairly often* and *frequently*.

Taken together, the results from the examination of the MLQ-5X transformational leadership scores by participant and the SL-ASIA cultural behavior score by participant, an indication that participants exhibit transformational leadership styles/practices as defined by the Multifactor Leadership Questionnaire (MLQ-5X) exhibits a cultural behavior score as well. After further examination on the previous research questions, it has been observed that a qualitative component in the research questions is necessary. If the researcher would do this study again, a third research question with a qualitative nature would be included to enhance the triangulation design and to elaborate additional analysis by participant. This additional research questions and analysis would be as follows:

## Research Question 3

*What are the self-perceptions of leadership determined by the qualitative scores and frequencies obtained from the interviews for the business leaders that exhibit a transformational leadership style/practices as defined by the Multifactor Leadership Questionnaire (MLQ-5X)?*

The findings from the qualitative data collection in Phase Two are evidence that the leaders that exhibit a transformational leadership style/practices as defined by the Multifactor Leadership Questionnaire (MLQ-5X), exhibit transformational leadership attributes and behaviors as well, from the self-perceptions of leadership determined by the qualitative scores and frequencies from interviews.

## Hypothesis

Hypothesis 1 stated that a relationship exists between acculturation scores determined by the Suinn-Lew Asian Self Identity Acculturation scale (SL-ASIA) and the transformational leadership style/practices of the business leaders as defined by the Multifactor Leadership Questionnaire (MLQ-5X).

Based on the findings previously discussed and interpreted, Hypothesis 1 was supported. The findings summarized in the quantitative analysis, as well as the findings condensed in the qualitative analysis provided substantiate evidence that a relationship exists between acculturation scores determined by the Suinn-Lew Asian Self Identity Acculturation scale (SL-ASIA) and the transformational leadership style/practices of the business leaders as defined by the Multifactor Leadership Questionnaire (MLQ-5X).

The findings displayed at the Correlation results for MLQ-5X Transformational, SL-ASIA, and Demographics reported that a statistically significant relationship was identified between the Suinn-Lew Asian Self Identity Acculturation scale (SL-ASIA) and the

Multifactor Leadership Questionnaire (MLQ-5X) transformational factors. Cultural Behaviors score and Idealized Influence-Attributes (IIA) were positively related (r = 0.886, p < 0.01). As scores for the SL-ASIA questionnaire increased, scores for the IIA also increased significantly. Conversely, the remaining correlations between the Suinn-Lew Asian Self Identity Acculturation scale (SL-ASIA) and the Multifactor Leadership Questionnaire (MLQ-5X) for transformational factors, were not statistically significant, ranging from -0.411 to 0.675. The findings from the qualitative analysis, reported that 90% of participants exposed an Idealized Attributes (IIA), as they have gone beyond self-interest for the good of the group in their job. Although not significant, it is interesting to note that the interview analysis uncovered that the highest frequency of participants' self-perceptions is Intellectual Stimulation (IS), with a 100% frequency, followed by Inspirational Motivation (IM), with a 90% frequency of Transformational Leadership Attributes and Behaviors. The findings from the triangulation of quantitative and qualitative analysis revealed that Idealized Attributes (IIA), a transformational trait, associated favorable.

The findings summarized at the MLQ-5X and SL-ASIA Quantitative Scores by Participant reported by participant that the relationship between acculturation scores determined by the Suinn-Lew Asian Self Identity Acculturation scale (SL-ASIA) and the transformational leadership style/practices of the business leaders as defined by the Multifactor Leadership Questionnaire (MLQ-5X) is significant, as the participants who exhibit transformational leadership primarily revealed a cultural behavior mean (r = 2.13), implying that the respondents were not in a low acculturation score, meaning that they are not high Asian identification, or in a high acculturation score. Participant P1 (r = 1.67) was slightly low in acculturation, and P5 (r = 3.48) was slightly high in acculturation from the mean.

The participants who exhibited transformational leadership during the quantitative analysis in Phase One, provided during Phase Two during the interview sufficient evidence to support their leadership style.

## *Implications*

Based on the findings of this research study, there are two main implications for further research and study. First, as China and the United States business cooperation intensifies, the core cultural values of the Chinese business leaders will continue changing in an unpredictable fashion. The Chinese business leaders, participants in this study, exhibited a combination of Asian-Western identification scores and a mixture of beliefs in Asian values as well as American values. Their Behavioral Competencies showed that they fit very well and generally fit with other Asians; concurrently, they generally fit and fit very well with other Americans who are non-Asian. In brief, the finding suggested that a Chinese business leader in this study can hold their Asian values, yet fit with American values and view themselves as a blend of both. A broader representation of Chinese business leaders will provide more insight to this point. A larger sample would allow the researcher to stratify participants in different age groups that allow a better observation of the acculturation process.

It would be an inaccuracy to conclude that the cultural values and behaviors of Chinese business leaders living and working in the United States are likely to become Western oriented or individualistic due to the fact that they are exposed to the American culture. A junction of values associated with Western business practices and their own cultural values is the possible outcome.

A cross-cultural investigation of work values among young executives in China and the United States completed by Pan et al., 2010, concurred with the findings in this study. The study investigated what values were important to young American and Chinese Managers and explored if the ethical values of young executives in different countries are converging to a common global business culture. The general conclusions revealed that Chinese executives are likely to hold values that are similar to United States managers, however, are also likely to be culturally bound to their own collectivistic values such as family and hierarchy (Pan et al., 2010). The study further explained that the Chinese managers have two cultural influences—tradition and Western- crossvergence (Ralston, Gustafson, Cheung, & Terpstra, 1993), as cited in Pan et al., 2010. Ralston et al., 1993 stated that crossvergence means that the Chinese internalized some aspects of the Western individualism into their Confucian-based value system. Pan et al., 2010, study further concluded that the Confucian traits of listening, flexibility, self control, and discipline could prove beneficial to Western managers to follow in negotiations with their Chinese counterparts.

In the same fashion, Kwon (2012) compared regional differences in the work-related values of Chinese employees, using Hofstede's cultural dimensions, indicating individualism scores. The findings suggested that in terms of individualism, uncertainty avoidance, and long-term orientation, statistically significant differences were found across the regions of Shenzhen and Taiyuan. Taiyuan scored higher than Shenzhen on long-term orientation, yet Shenzhen scored higher on individualism and uncertainty avoidance than did Taiyuan (Kwon, 2012). According to Kwon (2012), China's recent rapid economic development from an agricultural to an industrial economy is positively correlated with uncertainty avoidance, and the region of Shenzhen has become a successful economic area with international influence.

Second, as the world continues its route to a global economy and the demand for business leaders with worldwide competences increases, new leadership styles are needed and new leadership trends will continue to evolve. The rise of globalization spurred the need to acquire transformational leaders (Avolio & Bass, 2004). The latest and most promising phase of leadership theory is transformational leadership (Van Seters & Field, 1993) because it is useful and valuable in producing and maintaining organizational changes. Transformational leadership and collectivistic cultures are linked, and transformational leadership processes are most likely to be enhanced in collectivistic cultures (Jung et al., 1995). In fact, since transformational leaders ask followers to surpass their own self-interest for the good of the group, organization, or society; to consider their long-term needs to develop themselves, rather than their immediate needs; and to become more aware of what is really important, followers are converted into leaders (Burns, 1978). Jung and Avolio (1999) evaluated transactional and transformational leadership styles. For individual and group-task conditions the end products were compared, and whether a different impact on individualists and collectivists carrying out brainstorming tasks could be found were evaluated. This study found that collectivist groups generate more ideas with a transformational leader, while the individualists produced additional ideas with a transactional leader. According to Avolio and Bass (2004), "the mutual obligation in collectivist societies between leaders and followers facilitates the transformational leader's *individualized consideration*" (p. 41). Consequently, it is even more important for leaders in collectivist societies such as China to produce opportunities that enhance transformational leadership styles.

The findings from the triangulation of quantitative and qualitative analysis in this study suggested that Idealized Attributes (IIA), was significant related; participants exposed this trait, as they have gone beyond self-interest for the good of the group on their job. In fact, a leader with idealized influence-attributed instills pride in others for being associated with him (her), goes beyond self-interest for the good of the group, acts in ways that build others' respect for him (her), and displays a sense of power and confidence (Avolio & Bass, 2004). Also, as explained by Waldman and Bass (1986), Howell and Avolio (1993), and Waldman et al. (1990), transformational leadership does not replace transactional leadership; in fact, transformational leaders can be transactional when suitable. Bass (1985) suggested that transformational leadership augments transactional leadership in achieving the goals of the leader, associate, group, and organization.

The Chinese business leaders who participate in this study exhibit transformational leadership styles and behaviors as well as transactional leadership style and behaviors, suggesting that the Chinese business leader's leadership style, although influenced by Western and European styles of leadership, continue to maintain basic Confucian ideals and values. The Chinese business leader's leadership style appears to adapt and fit to the newer models of global leadership. Once again, a broader representation of Chinese business leaders will provide more insight to this point. A larger sample would allow the researcher to assess participants in their different leadership styles.

## *Recommendations*

The acculturation scale is not exclusive for Chinese population, thus the design of a specific scale exclusively for Chinese population that allowed a more accurate acculturation assessment and understanding of the Chinese business leaders is needed. The use of one scale for all Asian groups may not reflect the cultural styles and behaviors of a specific group (Suinn et al., 1987) because the Chinese from mainland China hold on more to their traditional Chinese culture than the Chinese from Taiwan, Hong Kong, and Singapore, which are more democratic and Westernized than mainland China (Yu and Berryman 1996).

Further, a more significant representation of participants will enhance the studies of leadership and acculturation of Chinese business leaders in America. Samples with different education, age, and job category levels will provide more insight to leadership and acculturation research.

## *Areas for Further Research*

Leadership and acculturation are a phenomenon that has been studied for centuries; yet, the study and/or correlation of leadership and Chinese business leaders' acculturation in the United States relationship has not received enough or any attention. The search for leadership and acculturation of Chinese business leaders in the

United States did not match any articles or find any results. Chinese acculturation studies in the United States are mainly focused on social (family, parenting, child, elderly, etc.), psychological, religious, health, and educational subjects. Conversely, the explosion in cross-cultural leadership issues faced by governments, economies, organizations, and leaders, in the last decades, due to the globalization of the economy and the new economy trends, has made the study of leadership and culture an important topic. There are literally millions of cross-cultural leadership studies in recent research. A simple Google exploration showed 28-plus million results, and in a more selective search in a dissertation and thesis database, the research provided 68-plus thousand results. Furthermore, China-United States, and United States-China economy studies have had an explosion in the last decades, mostly due to China's economy spot in the world at this moment in time.

Therefore, the researcher recommended for further studies the investigation of the relationship between acculturation and leadership style/practices of Chinese business leaders living and working in the United States. Furthermore, the researcher recommended that new studies incorporate larger populations representing more areas of Chinese population in the United States, as well as a broader spectrum of companies that represent a larger number of sectors of the United States economy.

## Conclusion

It is important to understand relevant cultural differences because the most suitable leadership styles, organizational structures, and management practices will vary across cultures (Hofstede, 1997). The current lack of literature on the relationship between acculturation and leadership for Chinese business leaders in the United States places this study in a unique perspective to establish new ground based on its empirical findings.

# Bibliography

Alon, I., & Shenkar, O. (2003). *Chinese culture, organizational behavior, and international business management.* Santa Barbara, CA: Greenwood.

Antonakis, J. (2001). The validity of the transformational, transactional, & laissez-faire leadership model as measured by the Multifactor Leadership Questionnaire (MLQ 5X). Ph.D. dissertation, Walden University, United States -- Minnesota. Retrieved November 23, 2010, from ABI/INFORM Global. (Publication No. AAT 3000380).

Ardichvili, A., & Kuchinke, K. P. (2002). Leadership styles & cultural values among managers and subordinates: A comparative study of four countries of the former Soviet Union, Germany, and the US. *Human Resource Development International, 5,* 99-117. Doi: 10.1080/136788601 10046225

Avolio, B. & Bass, B. (2004). *Multifactor leadership questionnaire* (3rd ed.). Mind Garden, Inc.

Avolio, B., Bass, B., Walumbwa, F. O., & Zhu, W. (2004). *MLQ Multifactor leadership questionnaire* (3rd ed.). Manual & Sampler Set. Redwood, CA: Mind Garden.

Avolio, B. J. (1999) *Full Leadership Development: Building the Vital Forces in Organizations.* Thousand Oaks, CA: Sage.

Avolio, B. J., Walderman, D. A., & Yanimarina, F. J. (1991). Leading in the 1990s: The four is of transformational leadership. *Journal of European Industrial Training, 15*, 9-16.

Bachman, D. (1992). *The limits on leadership in China.* Asian Survey, 32, 1046-1062.

Bailey, P. J. (2001). *China in the Twentieth Century* (2nd ed.). Blackwell, Malden, MA.

Ball, P. (2004). *The essence of Tao.* London: Arturus.

Bass, B. M. (1985). *Leadership and performance beyond expectations.* New York, NY: The Free Press.

Bass, B. M. (1990). *Bass and Stogdill's handbook of leadership: Theory, research and managerial applications* (3rd ed.). New York, NY: The Free Press.

Bass, B. M. (1997). Does the transactional-transformational leadership paradigm transcend organizational and national boundaries? *The American Psychologist Journal, 52,* 130-139.

Bass, B., & Avolio, B. (1994). *Improving organizational effectiveness through transformational leadership.* Thousand Oaks, CA: Sage.

Bass, B. M., & Avolio, B. J. (1995). The Multifactor Leadership Questionnaire (form R, revised). Palo Alto, CA: Mind Garden, Inc.

Berry, J. W. 1980. Acculturation as Varieties of Adaptation. In Acculturation: Theory, Models and Some New Findings, ed. A. Padilla, 9-25. Boulder:Westview.

Biesta, G. (2007). Education and the democratic person: Towards a political conception of democratic education. *Teachers College Record, 109,* 740-769.

Boisot, M., & Child, J. 1996. *From fiefs to clans and network capitalism: Explaining China's emerging economic order.* Admin. Sci. Quart. 41 600-628.

Bond, M. H. (1991). *Beyond the Chinese face: Insights from psychology.* Hong Kong, People's Republic of China: Oxford University Press.

Bond, M. H., & Hwang, K. K. (1986). The social psychology of Chinese people. In M. H. Bond (Ed.), *The psychology of Chinese people* (pp. 213-266). Oxford, UK: Oxford University Press.

Brodbeck, F. C., Frese, M., Akerblom, S., Audia, G., Bakacsi, G., Bendova, H., et al. (2000) Cultural variation of leadership prototypes across 22 European countries. *Journal of Occupational and Organizational Psychology, 73,* 1-29.

Brousseau, K., Ho, J., & Tseng, C. (2005). *Leadership development will spur China's Global market expansion.* Los Angeles: Korn/Ferry international.

Burns, J. M. (1978). *Leadership.* New York, NY: Harper & Row.

Byham, W. (2009). Developing the next generation of Chinese business leaders. *The China Business Review, 6,* 28-33.

Carless, S. A. (1998). Assessing the discriminant validity of transformational leader behaviour as measured by the MLQ. *Journal of Occupational & Organizational Psychology, 71*(4), 353-358.

CCL - Center for Creative Leadership. (2010). Research Projects - World Leadership Survey. May 20, 2010 http://www.ccl.org/leadership/research/worldSurvey.aspx

CCTV-China Central Television. (2010, March 7). Third Session of the 11th National People's Congress (NPC) [Televison Broadcast]. Beijing, China: CCTV

Central Intelligence Agency. (2010). World factbook China. Retrieved from https://www.cia.gov/library/publications/the-world-factbook/geos/ch.html

Chan, K. Y., & Drasgow, F. (2001). Toward a theory of individual differences and leadership: Understanding the motivation to lead. *Journal of Applied Psychology, 86,* 481-498.

Chao, E. (2007). Back to school. *China International Business, 239,* 18-25.

Chao, R., & Tseng, V. (2002). Prenting of Asians. In M. H. Bomstein (Ed.), *Handbook of parenting: Vol. 4, Social conditions and applied parenting* (pp. 59-93). Mahwah, NJ: Lawrence Erlbaum.

Chemers, M. M. (2002). Meta-cognitive, social, and emotional intelligence of transformational leadership: Efficacy and effectiveness. In R. E. Riggio, S. E. Murphy, & F. J. Pirozzolo (Eds.), *Multiple intelligences and leadership* (pp. 225-245). Mahwah, NJ: Lawrence Erlbaum.

Chen, M. (2004). *Asian management systems: Chinese, Korean and Japanese style of Business.* Mason: Cengage learning.

Chen, S. (2002). Son of heaven and Son of God: Interactions among ancient Asiatic cultures regarding sacral kingship and theophoric names. *Journal of the Royal Asiatic Society, 12,* 289-325.

Cheng, L. (2001). *China's leaders-The new generation.* Oxford, UK: Rowman & Littlefield.

Cheng, L. (2005). *The rise of China's yuppie corps: Top CEOs to watch* (Issue Brief No.14). China Leadership Monitor, 14. Retrieved from http://media.hoover.org/documents/clm14_lc.pdf

Child, J., & Rodrigues, S. (2005). Internalization of Chinese firms: A case of theoretical extension. *Journal of Management and Organization Review 1*(3), 381-340.

Chow, G. (2007). *China's economic transformation.* Boston, MA: Blackwell.

CNN, (2012) Obama takes key battlegrounds to win re-election. Posted: 11/07/2012 Retrieved: http://www.cnn.com/2012/11/06/politics/election-2012/

Conger, J. A., & Kanungo, R. N. (1987). Toward a behavioral theory of charismatic leadership in organizational settings. *Academy of Management Review, 12,* 637-647.

Creel, H. G. (1974). Shen Pu-hai: A Chinese political philosopher of the fourth century B.C.E. Chicago, IL: University of Chicago Press.

Davis, D. D., & Bryant, J. L. (2003). *Influence at a distance: Leadership in global virtual teams.* In W. H. Mobley & P. W. Dorfman (Eds.), *Advances in Global Leadership, 3,* 303-340. Oxford, UK: JAL.

Den Hartog, D. N., Van Muijen, J. J., & Koopman, P. L. (1997). Transactional verses transformational leadership: An analysis of the MLQ. *Journal of Occupational and Organizational Psychology, 70*(1), 19.34.

Deng, L., & Gibson P. (2008). A qualitative evaluation on the role of. cultural intelligence in cross-cultural leadership effectiveness. *International Journal of Leadership Studies, 3,* 181-197.

Dorfman, P. W., & Howell J. P. (1988). *Dimensions of national culture and effective leadership patterns.* Hofstede revisited. *Advances in International and Comparative Management, 3,* 127-150.

Dorfman, P. W., & Howell, J. P. (1997). Managerial leadership in the United States and Mexico: Distant neighbors or close cousins. In C. S. Granrose & S. Oskamp (Eds.), *Cross cultural workgroups* (pp. 234-264). Thousand Oaks, CA: Sage.

Duan, C., and Vu, P. 2000. Acculturation of Vietnamese Students Living In or Away from Vietnamese Communities. *Journal of Multicultural Counseling and Development,* 28(4), 225-41.

Egri, C., & Ralston, D. (2004). Generation cohorts and personal values: A comparison of China and the United States. *Organization Science, 15*(2), 210-220. doi:10.1287/orsc.1030.0048.

EXPO 2010 Shanghai China. (2008). Brief introduction of World Expo Shanghai. Retrieved from http://en.expo2010.cn/a/20081116/000004.htm

Fan, Y. (1995, December). Chinese cultural values and entrepreneurship: A preliminary consideration. Durham University Business School. Paper presented at the Sixth ENDEC World Conference on Entrepreneurship, Shanghai China.

Farh, J., & Cheng B. (2000). *Management and organizations in the Chinese context: A cultural analysis of paternalistic leadership in chinese organizations.* New York, NY: Palgrave MacMillan.

Fernandez, J. A., & Underwood, L. (2006). *China CEO: Voices of experience from 20 international business leaders.* New York, NY: John Wiley & Sons.

Flood, J. (2010). "Leadership Qualities for Extraordinary Leaders." Women's Resource Group, Siemens Energy Inc. Orlando, Florida. May 13, 2010.

Frey, M. (2007). Personality, lifestyle, and transformational leadership from a humanistic perspective. Ph.D. dissertation, Georgia State University, United States -- Georgia. Retrieved October 16, 2010, from ABI/INFORM Global.(Publication No. AAT 3272876).

Gagliardi, G. (1999). *Sun Tzu's art of war plus the ancient Chinese secret revealed.* Seattle, WA: Clearbridge.

Gagliardi, G. (2001). *Sun Tzu's art of war plus its amazing secrets: The keys to strategy.* Seattle, WA: Clearbridge.

Gagliardi, G. (2004). *Sun Tzu's art of war plus the warrior class: 306 lessons in strategy.* Seattle, WA: Clearbridge.

Gallo, F. (2011). *Business leadership in China: How to blend best Western practices with Chinese wisdom.* Hoboken, NJ: John Wiley & Sons.

Gallo, F. T. (2008). *Business leadership in China. How to blend Western practices with Chinese wisdom.* Singapore: Wiley.

Geletkanycz, M. A. (1997). The salience of "culture's consequences": The effects of cultural values on top executive commitment to the status quo. *Strategic Management Journal, 18,* 615-634.

Geyer, A. L. J., & Steyrer, J. M. (1998). Transformational leadership and objective performance in banks. *Applied Psychology: An international review, 47,* 397-420.

Gordon, M. (1964). *Assimilation in American life.* New York: Oxford University Press.

Grint, K. (2002). Management or leadership. *Journal of Health Services Research and Policy,* 248-251.

Grove, C. N. (2005). Overviews of the GLOBE research project on leadership worldwide. Retrieved from http://www.grovewell. com/pub-GLOBE-intro.html

Guthrie, D. (2006). *China and globalization: The social, and political transformation of Chinese society.* New York, NY: Routledge.

Hampden-Turner, C., & Trompenaars, F. (2000). *Building cross-cultural competence: How to create wealth from conflicting values.* New Haven, CT: Yale University Press.

Hartman, L. (1999). A psychological analysis of leadership effectiveness. *Strategy and Leadership, 27*(6), 30-32.

HayGroup. (2007). East meets west. Bridging two great business cultures. HayGroup. Retrieved from http://content.ll-0.com/ haygroup1/east.pdf?i=062707122034

Hazuda, H. P., Stern, M. P., & Haffner, S. M. (1988). Acculturation and assimilation among Mexican Americans: Sales and population-based data. *Social Science Quarterly, 69,* 687-706.

Heberer, T., & Gluckman, T. (2003). *Private entrepreneurs in China and Vietnam: Social and political functioning of strategic groups.* Boston, MA: Brill.

Heifetz, R. A. (1994). *Leadership without easy answers.* Cambridge, MA: Harvard University Press.

Hirahara, N. (2003). *Distinguished Asian American business Leaders.* Westport, CT: Greenwood Publishing Group.

Hofstede, G. (1980). *Culture's consequences: International differences in work-related values.* Newbury Park, CA: Sage.

Hofstede, G. (1994). Values Survey Module 1994. VSM 94. Retrieved on January 31, 2010, from http://stuwww.uvt.nl/~csmeets/~1st-VSM.html

Hofstede, G. (1997). *Cultures and organizations: Software of the mind.* McGraw-Hill, London.

Hofstede, G. (2001). *Culture's consequences* (2nd ed.). Thousand Oaks, CA: Sage.

Hofstede, G. (2001). *Culture's consequences, (Second Edition): Comparing values, behaviors, institutions and organizations across nations.* Thousand Oaks CA: Sage Publications.

Hofstede, G. (2007). Asian management in the 21st century. *Asia Pacific Journal of Management, 24,* 411-420.

House, R. J., Hanges, P. J., Javidan, M., Dorfman, P. W., & Gupta, V. (2004). *Culture, leadership, and organizations. The GLOBE study of 62 societies.* Thousand Oaks, CA: Sage.

House, R. J., Wright, N. S., & Aditya, R. N. (1997). *Cross-cultural research on organizational leadership: A critical analysis and a proposed theory.* In P. C. Earley & M. Erez (Eds.), *New perspective in international industrial organizational psychology* (pp. 535-625). San Francisco: New Lexington.

Howell, J. M., & Avolio, B. J. (1993). Transformational leadership, transactional leadership, locus of control, and support for innovation: Key predictors of consolidated business business unit performance. *Journal of Applied Psychology, 78,* 891-902.

Hu, H. (2002, October 18). *Family planning law and China's birth control situation.* China Daily, Retrieved from http://www.chinadaily.com.cn/china/2010npc/2010-03/12/content_9581819.htm.

Hwang, K.-K. (1997). Guanxi and Mientze: Conflict resolution in Chinese society. In G.-M. Chen (Ed.), *Chinese conflict management and resolution* (pp. 17-42). San Antonio, TX: International Association for Intercultural Communication Studies, Trinity University.

Iwuh, P. (2010). Leadership at NEEDS: A study of the frequency in which leaders at the Nigerian National Economic and Empowerment Development Strategy (NEEDS) exhibit transformational leadership characteristics as measured by the Multifactor Leadership Questionnaire. Ph.D. dissertation, Capella University, United States -- Minnesota. Retrieved October 2, 2010, from Dissertations & Theses: Full Text. (Publication No. AAT 3396976).

Jin, Z. (2010, February 25). Rural population could drop to 400m. *China Daily*, p. 3.

Jones, H. (2010). *ChinAmerica: The uneasy partnership that will change the world.* New York: McGraw-Hill.

Jung, D. B., & Avolio, B. J. (1999). Effects of leadership style and followers' cultural orientation on performance in group and individual task conditions. *The Academy of Management Journal, 42,* 208-218.

Jung, D. I., Bass, B. M, & Sosik, J. J. (1995). Bridging leadership and culture: A theoretical consideration of transformational leadership and collectivistic cultures. *The Journal of Leadership Studies, 2*(4), 3-18.

Kanungo, R., & Mendonça, M. (1996). *Ethical dimensions of leadership.* Thousand Oaks, CA: Sage.

Keller, T. (1999). Images of the familiar: Individual differences and implicit leadership theories. *The Leadership Quarterly, 10,* 589-607.

Kinge, J., McGregor, R., Pilling, D., Dickie, M., & Authers, J. (2010, March). The financial times great debate: China will be a superpower by 2020 (Debate conducted at Shanghai International Literary Festival 2010). Shanghai, China.

Koh, W. L., Steers, R. M., & Terborg, J. R. (1995). The effects of transformational leadership on teacher attitudes and student performance in Singapore. *Journal of Organisational Behavior, 16,* 319.333.

Kouzes, J. M., & Posner, B. Z. (2007). *The leadership challenge.* San Francisco, CA: Jossey Bass.

Krug, B., & Pólos, L. (2000). The strawberry growth underneath the nettle: The emergence of entrepreneurs in China. Retrieved from http://repub.eur.nl/publications/eco_man/jel/p/index/213325832/

Kuchinke, K. P. (1999). Leadership and culture: Work-related values and leadership styles among one company's U.S. and German telecommunication employees. *Human Resource Development Quarterly, 10*(2), 135-154. Retrieved November 10, 2010, from ABI/INFORM Global. (Document ID: 42916678).

Kuhn, R. L. (2010). *How China's leaders think.* Singapore, China: Wiley.

Kwon, J. (2012). Does China have more than one culture? *Asia Pacific Journal of Management, 29*(1), 79-102. doi:10.1007/s10490-010-9191-y

Kynge, J. (2006). *China Shakes The World. A Titan's Rise and Troubled Future and The Challenge For America.* Boston - New York: A Mariner Book. Houghton Mifflin Company.

Ladany, L. 1988. *The Communist Party of China and Marxism (1921-1985).* Hong Kong University Press, Hong Kong.

LaFromboise, T., Coleman, J., & Gerton, J. (1993). Psychological impact of biculturalism: Evidence and theory. *Psychological Bulletin, 114,* 395-412.

Laurent, A. (1983). The cultural diversity of Western conceptions of management. *International Studies of Management and Organization, 13*(2), 75-96.

Leslie, J. B., & Van Velsor, E. (1998). *A cross-national comparison of effective leadership and teamwork: Toward a global workforce.* Greensboro, NC: Center for Creative Leadership.

Liao, W. K (1939). *The complete works of Han Fei Tzu: Vol. 1.* London, UK: Arthur Probsthain.

Liu, W. L. (2008). *KFC in China.* Singapore: Wiley.

Livermore, D. (2011). *The Cultural Intelligence Difference.* Amacom. NewYork

Lowe, S. (2003). Business culture and management theory. In I. Alon & O. Shenkar (Eds.), *Chinese culture, organizational behavior and international business management.* Santa Barbara, CA: Greenwood.

Luthans, F. (2005). *Organizational Behavior.* Boston, MA: McGraw-Hill Irwin.

Magala, S. (2005). *Cross-cultural competence.* London, England: Routledge.

Malaghan, T. (2012) How To Segment the Hispanic Market by Acculturation. Retrieved http://stevensonfinancialmarketing.wordpress.com/2012/09/29/how-to-segment-the-hispanic-market-by-acculturation/

Malik, R. (1997). *Chinese entrepreneurs in the economic development of China*. Westport, CT: Greenwood.

Mendenhall, M. E. (2006). The elusive, yet critical challenge of developing global leaders. *European Management Journal, 24*, 422-429.

Meredith, C. (2008). *The relationship of emotional intelligence and transformational leadership behavior in non-profit executive leaders*. Ph.D. dissertation, Capella University, United States -- Minnesota. Retrieved October 16, 2010, from Accounting and Tax Periodicals. (Publication No. AAT 3290654).

Michaelson, G. A. (2001). *Sun Tzu. The art of war for managers. 50 strategic rules*. Avon, MA: Adams Media.

Mind Garden. (2010). Company background. Retrieved from http://www.mindgarden.com/about.htm

Mizokawa, D. T., & Ryckman, D. B. (1990). Attributions of academic success and failure: A comparison of six Asian-American ethnic groups. *Journal of Cross-Cultural Psychology, 21*, 434-451.

Naughton, B. (2007). *The Chinese economy: Transitions and growth*. Cambridge, MA: The MIT Press.

Oetting, E. R., & Beauvais, F. (1991). Orthogonal cultural identification theory: The cultural identification of minority adolescents. *The International Journal of the Addictions, 25*, 655-685.

Oh, T. K. (1991). Understanding managerial values and behavior among the gang of four: South Korea, Taiwan, Singapore and Hong Kong. *Journal of Management Development, 10*, 46-56.

Pan, Y., Song, X., Goldschmidt, A., & French, W. (2010). A cross-cultural investigation of work values among young executives in china and the USA. *Cross Cultural Management, 17*(3), 283-298. doi:10.1108/13527601011068379

Park, S. H., & Vanhonacker, W. R. (2007). The challenge of multinational corporations in China: Think local, act global. MIT Sloan Management Review. Retrieved from http://sloanreview.mit.edu/the-magazine/articles/2007/summer/48402/the-challenge-for-multinational-corporations-in-china-think-local-act-global

Pedersen, P., & Connerley, M. (2005). *Leadership in a diverse and multicultural environment: Developing awareness, knowledge, and skills.* Thousand Oaks, CA: Sage.

Pellegrini, E. K., & Scandura, T. A. (2008). Paternalistic leadership: A review and agenda for future research. *Journal of Management, 34,* 566-593.

Perkowski, J. (2008). *Managing the dragon: How I'm building a billion-dollar business in China.* New York, NY: Crown Business.

Pfeifer, D., & Love, M. (2004). Leadership in Aotearoa NewZealand: A cross-cultural study. Retrieved from http://www.prismjournal.org/fileadmin/Praxis/Files/Journal_Files/Pfeifer_Love.pdf

Pillai, R., & Meindl, J. R. (1998). Context and charisma: A "meso" level examination of the relationship of organic structure, collectivism, and crisis to charismatic leadership. *Journal of Management, 24,* 643-671.

Plucker, J. A. (1994). Issues in the social and emotional adjustment and development of a gifted, Chinese American student. *Roeper Review, 17,* 89-95.

Pye, L. W. (1991). Political culture revisited. *International Society of Political Psychology, 12,* 487-508.

Ralston, D. A., Gustafson, D. J., Cheung, F., & Terpstra, R. H. (1993). Differences in managerial values: A study of US, Hong Kong and PRC managers. *Journal of International Business Studies, 24*(2), 249-75.

Ralston, D., Holt, D., Terpstra, R., & Cheng, Y. (2007). The impact of national culture and economic ideology on managerial work values: A study of the United States, Russia, Japan, and China. *Journal of International Business Studies, 39,* 47-52.

Real state. (2010, March 1). *Shanghai Daily,* p. B7

Redding, G., & Wong, Y. Y. (1986). The psychology of Chinese organizational behavior. In M. H. Bond (Ed.), *The psychology of the Chinese people* (pp. 267-295). New York, NY: Oxford Press.

Robie, C., Johnson, K. M., Nilsen, D., & Hazucha, J. F. (2001). The right stuff: Understanding cultural differences in leadership performance. *Journal of Management Development, 20,* 639-649.

Robinson, G. H. (1993). A study of the relationship of leadership styles of principals and teacher job satisfaction (Unpublished doctoral dissertation). University of Arkansas, Fayetteville.

Rosen, S. 1990. The impact of reform policies on youth attitudes. D. Davis, E. F. Vogel (Eds.). Chinese Society on the Eve of Tiananmen: The Impact of Reform. Harvard University Press, Cambridge, MA, 283-374.

Rost, J. C. (1993). Leadership development in the new millennium. *The Journal of Leadership Studies, 1,* 91-110.

Sanders, J., Hopkins, W., & Geroy, G. (2003). From transactional to transcendental: Toward an integrated theory of leadership. *Journal of Leadership and Organizational Studies, 9,* 21-31.

Schell, O. (1994). *Mandate of heaven: In China, a new generation of entrepreneurs, dissidents, bohemians and technocrats lays claim to China's future.* New York, NY: Simon & Schuster

Seltzer, J., & Bass, B. M. (1990). Transformational leadership: Beyond initiation and consideration. *Journal of Management, 16,* 693-703.

Shambaugh, D. (1993). Introduction: The emergence of "greater China." *The China Quarterly, 136,* 653-659.

Sheh, S. W. (2002). Behavioural attributes of the transformational Chinese leader (Unpublished doctoral dissertation). Retrieved from ProQuest Information and Learning Company. (UMI No. 3047749)

Shen, D. (2010). EXPO: Raising China's soft power. Retrieved from http://www.china.org.cn/opinion/2010-05/07/content_19994928.htm

Shi, T. (2000). Cultural values and democracy in the People's Republic of China. *The China Quarterly, 162,* 540-559.

Siemens. (2010). Siemens in China Profiles. Retrieved December 14, 2010, from http://w1.siemens.com.cn/pdf/Siemens-in-China_en.pdf

Siemens. (2010a). China. Retrieved from http://www.siemens.com/about/en/worldwide/china_1154598.htm

Siemens. (2010b). China News. Retrieved from http://info.siemens.com.cn/SLC/news/press/2010_02_02_01.asp

Siu, A. M. H., & Shek, D. T. L. (2005). Psychometric properties of the Chinese family assessment instrument in Chinese adolescents in Hong Kong. *Adolescence, 40,* 817-830.

Smither, J. W., London, M., & Richmond, K. (2005). The relationship between leaders' personality and their reactions to and use of multisource feedback: A longitudinal study. *Group and Organization Management, 30,* 181-210.

Stanford Encyclopedia of Philosophy. (2006). Confucius. Retrieved from http://plato.stanford.edu/entries/confucius

Stone, A. G., & Patterson, K. (2005). The history of leadership focus. Paper presented at the Servant Leadership Research Roundtable. Retrieved from http://www.regent.edu/acad/global/publications/sl_proceedings/2005/stone_history.pdf

Strategic Management (Ed.). (2005, June 1). The changing face of management in China. Retrieved from http://knowledge.wharton.upenn.edu/index.cfm?fa=viewarticle &ID=1164: Knowledge@Wharton.

Sue, S., & Okazaki, S. (1990). Asian-American educational achievements: A phenomenon in search of an explanation. *The American Psychologist, 45,* 913-920.

Suinn, R. M., Ahuna, C., Khoo, G. (1992). The Suinn-Lew Asian Self-Identity Acculturation scale: Concurrent and factorial validation. *Educational and Psychological Measurement, 52*(4), 1041-1046.

Suinn, R. M., Rickard-Figueroa, K., Lew, S., & Vigil, P. (1987). The Suinn-Lew Asian Self-Identity Acculturation Scale: An initial report. *Educational and Psychological Measurement, 47,* 401-407.

Swidler, A. (1986). Culture in action: Symbols & strategies. *American Sociological Review, 51,* 273-286.

Tess Lyons. (2005, October). Where East meets West. China Staff, 11(9), 34-36. Retrieved September 11, 2010, from ABI/INFORM Global. (Document ID: 926575211).

Thornton, J. L. (2008). Long time coming: The prospects of democracy in China. *Foreign Affairs, 87,* 2-22.

Tian, X. 1998. *Dynamics of Development in an Opening Economy: China Since 1978*. Nova Science Publishers, Commack, NY.

Tichy, N. M., & Devanna, M. A. (1986). *The transformational leader*. New York, NY. John Wiley and Sons.

Tracey, J. B., & Hinkin, T. R. (1994). Transformational leaders in the hospitality industry. *Cornell Hotel and Restaurant Administration Quarterly, 35*(2), 18-24.

Tsai, J.L., Ying, Y., & Lee, P.A. (2000). The meaning of "being Chinese" and "being American": Variation among Chinese American young adults. Journal of Cross-Cultural Psychology, 31, 302-322.

Trompenaars, F. (1993). *Riding the waves of culture: Understanding cultural diversity in business*. London, UK: Breatley.

Van Seters, D. A., & Field, R. H. (1993). The evolution of leadership theory. *Journal of Organizational Change Management, 3*, 29-45.

Van Wart, M. (2003). Public sector leadership theory: An assessment. *Public Administration Review*, 214-228

Vohra, R. 2000. *China's Path to Modernization: A Historical Review From 1800 to the Present*. Prentice-Hall, Upper Saddle River, NJ.

Wah, S. S. (2002). Behavioral attributes of the transformational Chinese leader. Dissertation Abstracts International. (UMI No. 3047749)

Wakeman, F., & Wakeman, L. (2009). *Telling Chinese history: A selection of essays*. Los Angeles: University of California Press.

Waldman, D. A., & Bass, B. M. (1986). Adding to leader and follower transactions: The augmenting effect of transformational leadership (Working Paper No. 86-109). Binghamton: State University of New York, School of Management.

Waldman, D. A., Bass, B. M., & Yammarino, F. J. (1990). Adding to contingent-reward behavior: The augmenting effect of charismatic leadership. *Group and Organizational Studies, 15,* 381-394.

Watson, B. (1964). *Han Fei Tzu: Basic writings.* New York, NY: Columbia University Press.

Williams, G. (2014) Organization & Leadership Transformation. Retrieved from Outwardlooking.com

Wong, R. S. (2008). *Chinese entrepreneurship in a global era.* New York, NY: Taylor & Francis Inc.

Wren, J. T. (1995). *The leaders companion: Insight on leadership through the ages.* New York: The Free Press.

Wright, N. (2009). China's emerging role in global outsourcing. *The China Business Review, 6,* 44-49.

Wu, J. (2005). *China's long march toward a market economy.* Shanghai: Long River Press.

Xing, F. 1995. The Chinese cultural system: Implications for cross-cultural management. *SAM Advanced Management J., 60,* 14-20.

Xu, A., Xie, X., Liu, W., Xia, Y., & Liu, D. (2007). Chinese family strengths and resilience. *Marriage and Family Review, 41,* 143-164.

Yao, S. 2000. Economic development and poverty reduction in China over 20 years of reforms. *Economic Development and Cultural Change, 48,* 447-474.

Yasheng, H. (1990). Web of interests and patterns of behaviour of Chinese local economic bureaucracies and enterprises during reforms. *The China Quarterly, 12,* 431-458.

Yee, B. W. K., Debaryshe, B. D., Yuen, S., Kim, S. Y., & McCubbin, H. I. (1998). Asian American and Pacific Islander families:

Resiliency and life-span socialization in a cultural context. In L. C. Lee & N. W. S. Zane (Eds.), *Handbook of Asian American Psychology* (pp. 69-86). Thousand Oaks, CA: Sage.

Yeh, C. J., Kim, A. B., Pituc, S. T., & Atkins, M. (2008). Poverty, loss, and resilience: The story of Chinese immigrant youth. *Journal of Counseling Psychology, 55,* 34-48.

Yeung, H. W. C. (2008). Hybrid capitalism: A new breed of Chinese entrepreneurship in a global era. In R. S. Wong (Ed.), *Chinese entrepreneurship in a global era* (pp. 29-51). New York, NY: Taylor & Francis.

Yi, J. J., & Ye, S. X. (2003). *The Haier way: The making of a Chinese business leader and a global brand.* New Jersey: Homa and Sekey Books.

Yukl, G. A. (2002). *Leadership in organizations* (5th ed.). Upper Saddle River, NJ: Prentice-Hall.

Zedong, M. (1966). *Quotations from Chairman Mao Tse Tung.* Beijing: Foreign Languages Press.

Zhang, W., & Alon, I. (Eds.). (2009). *Biographical dictionary of new Chinese entrepreneurs and business leaders.* New York: Edgar publishing Inc.

Zhao, D. (2009). The mandate of heaven and performance legitimation in historical and contemporary China. *American Behavioral Scientist, 53,* 416-433.

Zhao, S. (2008). *China-US relations transformed: Perspectives and strategic interactions.* New York: Routledge.